THE

CONGREGATIONAL

WAY OF LIFE

Arthur A. Rouner, Jr.

PRENTICE-HALL, INC.
Englewood Cliffs, N.J.

This book is dedicated to my father in the faith, and my friend in the ministry, who, while loving me because I am his son, gave me a heritage in the home, in the ministry, and in the Congregational Way, greater than he will ever know.

Library of Congress Catalog Card Number: 60-13800

Printed in the United States of America
16767—T

Foreword

Every earnest seeker after Christian truth, whether a layman or clergyman, will profit by the study of *The Congregational Way of Life*, in which Arthur A. Rouner, Jr., has dealt with the spirit of liberal Protestantism as exemplified by the free fellowship of Congregationalism.

With rare skill, Mr. Rouner has interpreted a vital facet of the Christian faith, Congregationalism, whose principles are of deep concern to many who see freedom fading in countless levels of life, globally. It is the best book I know for quick and intelligent reading in this important field.

In the course of his interpretation of Congregationalism, Mr. Rouner discusses the great Christian doctrines from the viewpoint of modern scholarship, presenting explanations compatible with today's knowledge and scientific research. He clarifies many controversial aspects of Congregationalism in his exposition of this phase of organized Christianity.

The Congregational Way of Life should not be considered a document in a controversy, although it is of special interest to every Congregationalist.

It is a valuable contribution to Christian thought, wholly apart from the specific situation which gave rise to its writing. It will appeal to everyone of any faith who has asked himself or others any one of these questions: "What is Congregationalism? What has it done? Where is it going?

Who are its adherents? What does it matter whether it survives? Why is its freedom so precious?

For four years I served as chairman of the Committee on Free Church Polity and Unity of the Congregational-Christian fellowship. Representing all Congregational viewpoints, this committee made a thorough study of Congregationalism, past and present. Mr. Rouner's picture of Congregationalism in this book is in complete accord with the findings of this committee. It is, therefore, much more than one man's opinion. For this reason, I am especially pleased and honored to have been asked to write this brief foreword.

L. WENDELL FIFIELD, D.D.

Claremont, California

Preface

Books should never be written simply for the sake of the writing. The only excuse for offering still another on the subject of Congregationalism is that increasingly, through the early years of my ministry, this one has been burning to be written.

The last decade has been a time of crisis in American Congregationalism. New hopes have been raised, new directions taken. Many among us have deeply believed that, to meet the exigencies of life in the mid-twentieth century, our "Way" has needed a greater authority, more definite standards, and firmer doctrine. Others have believed with equal sincerity that Congregationalism itself was being challenged: that should the new directions be taken, one of the great Reformation forms of church life would go out of existence.

And yet, through it all countless numbers of the people in our own churches have been asking, "But what *is* Congregationalism? What *do* we believe? What is different about a Congregational Church?" At the very time we have been most eager to venture into new forms of church life, we have least understood the uniqueness of the heritage we have!

As I have lived through this crisis-time, first as a boy growing up in a New England parsonage, and now as a parson with a people of my own to shepherd, and as I have known and talked, often for long hours, with men of both the dominant viewpoints in American Congregationalism today, it has seemed to me that on neither side was there real appreciation of the unique and utterly revolutionary character of Congregationalism at its best. Their watch-words were always "freedom" or "fellowship," but little more.

With this repeated experience in the background and with the insistent questions being raised continually by the people of the church I have served in the Berkshire hills of Massachusetts, it has become a growing conviction with me that this book had to be written. If it never reached beyond my own people in Williamsburg,—and now in Newton—it would be worth writing. Now the Savoy Tercentenary contest has given me the opportunity and provided the spur.

To the Savoy Committee, Prof. Matthew Spinka, Ph.D. of Hartford Seminary, the Rev. Wendell Fifield, D.D. of First Church, Los Angeles, and the Rev. Henry David Gray, Ph.D. of South Church, Hartford, who very kindly selected my manuscript for the Award, and who also gave invaluable help in suggesting revisions, I am greatly indebted.

I wish to record my appreciation also to Mrs. Claude Kennedy who, before her recent death, was long a member of the Executive Committees of both the General Council and the National Association of Congregational Churches. She and her family have contributed materially toward the Savoy Award.

Many people have helped to make this book possible. My wife has been unrelenting critic and editor, as well as inspiration. Through the kindness of my father-in-law, Truman S. Safford, his secretaries Mrs. Robert Hulit, Miss Dorothea Verbeek and Mrs. Owen Pendergast helped in typing the manuscripts, along with Mrs. Erol Bowie and Miss Helen Drake of Williamsburg. To all of these generous friends I extend my grateful thanks. Without their help I could never have even attempted a task so demanding as the writing of a book.

For what it may contribute to the on-going discussion of Congregationalism, and for such help as it may be to the people of the Congregational Way, I offer then this book. My prayer as I send it out, is that in some measure it may begin to answer, or at least to stimulate fresh thinking on the question of "What is the Congregational Way?"

Arthur A. Rouner, Jr.

Contents

The Forgotten Heritage

American Congregationalists look for their spiritual heritage to a tiny group of Christians who lived and worshipped in the town of Scrooby, England at the turn of the seventeenth century. We are fond of revering them as the "Pilgrim Fathers": courageous adventurers to an unknown coast, and founders of a new way of life—but that hardly tells the story.

Compared with the churches we know today that one was most unusual. It met in no imposing edifice with spire and organ, but in the old manor house of Scrooby. It had no public hour of worship called by the ringing of a bell, but a silent assembling when the time was right. It had not the protection of king and government, but lived in daily fear, not only of the state, but of fellow-Christians.

Who were these people, so different from us, whom we call our fathers? Why was their life what it was, and why did they become strangers and pilgrims in an alien land?

They lived the life they did because, for Christ's sake, they had become spiritual and social outcasts. This hardship had been thrust upon them because they were children of their age, an age of intellectual and spiritual tur-

1

moil and upheaval. Theirs was the age in which the Reformation split wide the once solid church of Western Christendom; when men were reading the Bible in their native tongue as if for the first time; when the sense of the living presence of Christ was stronger than it had been for centuries; and when men were beginning to grasp what their faith really meant for the first time since the early years of Christianity.

It was an exciting age: an age in which men began once more to take their lives into their own hands in order to stand for what they believed to be right. It was such a stand that the little congregation at Scrooby took, believing with all their hearts that this was God's will for them.

The Reformation *had* come to England, but not without a struggle that left its character quite a different thing from that of the Reformed churches of Switzerland and Germany. Where in those countries a strong sense of God's will made known in the Bible was understood as the supreme authority for Christians, in England the bishops remained, and with them the belief that, to be authoritative, the Bible must be interpreted *by* the bishops. Moreover, in England Elizabeth had been queen, and by the church that grew under her reign, she was recognized as its sole governor. She it was who governed its constitution, its doctrine, and its discipline; the bishops were her appointees, and every citizen of the realm was considered a Christian and a tax-paying member of this state church.

To many devoted Christians, such control by the monarch and such authority in the clergy seemed a bold usurping of the authority of Christ. A Christian church has the right, they said, to determine its affairs in obedience to Christ's will—not to the will of the monarch. "The Bible is our authority," was their claim, "and the Lord we know through the Bible!"

The growing number of those who cherished this Biblical authority, and who wished to strip away from England's church the remnants of human authority so long connected with Rome, called themselves "Puritans." They wished to "purify" the church. Their dream was to transform it from within. England's reformation, they felt, had not gone far enough, and so their hope was to establish in her church as much Puritan discipline and practice as they could, and then wait for the government to bring about further reformation.

But there were others who, although they shared the Puritan view of Holy Scripture, were nevertheless not content to wait. The kind of church they believed God demanded, they wanted immediately. These were called Separatists. They were willing to go so far as actually to separate themselves from the state church and to establish congregations of their own where they could worship freely as Christ led them to worship and not as the state told them.

These Separatists held to at least three principles which they believed to have been the essence of the New Testament Church. One was that the Church is composed of Christian people only—people who love the Lord and are earnestly trying to follow Him as disciples. In sixteenth century England the church was assumed to be synonymous with the nation. Every citizen of the realm was a member of the church. But the Separatists recognized only people consecrated to Christ as members of the church. For them, Christians were people "separated" apart to the work of Christ—otherwise the Church would become a secular institution ruled by the will of the world rather than the will of Christ.

They believed also that if every church is a gathering of Christians then Christ himself is their guide and governor, and that therefore they have the right of self-government, that they may be free to follow Him. As far as they were concerned the queen had no right to rule the church.

Finally, they believed that the privilege and duty of sharing in the church's government belonged to every member equally. The Separatists recognized no spiritual hierarchy from people to priests to bishops. The Church, in their eyes, was a family of equal brothers. They believed Christ demanded them to regard the Church this way, and that He called them to be a persecuted minority for the very purpose that His worship and the life of His Church might be purified.

In those years of ferment there were many such separatist congregations in England, beginning as early as 1567 when one group was seized and imprisoned for assembling to worship. One of the best known was that led by Robert Browne in Norwich in 1580.

When the little congregation at Scrooby called the learned and saintly John Robinson about 1604 to be its pastor, it was not alone in its separation from the Anglican Church. But like the others, it was so harried by persecution and the necessity to meet secretly in fear for their lives, that in 1607 and 1608 the whole congregation, led by Robinson and Elder Brewster, escaped to Holland, and in 1609 settled in Leyden.

And yet those early Congregationalists, despite their kindly reception in Holland, were Englishmen. They loved their land, and their customs, and their language and they feared to lose them if they stayed long among the Dutch. And so it was that after twelve years and many preparations, part of that Leyden congregation determined to sail for America, if the King would permit them, there to increase the realm both of England and of Christ.

William Bradford describes the sad but hopeful parting of those adventuring Christians when, at the little port of Delftshaven, they boarded the *Speedwell*:

> "So they left that goodly and pleasant city, which had been their resting place near twelve years, but they knew that they were pilgrims and looked not much on these things, but lifted up their eyes to the heavens, their dearest country, and quieted their spirits." [1]

The minister they loved so much had bid them farewell with his blessing, and had counselled them that "if God should reveal anything to them by any other instrument of His, to be ready to receive it, as ever they were to receive any truth by his ministry." "For," as Winslow wrote, "he was very confident that the Lord had more truth and light to break forth out of His Holy Word." [2]

This was the spirit in which the great adventure began. God was their guide, and they followed Him with open hearts, eager to do His will.

Part of John Robinson's advice was also that they should study the possibility of union with English Puritanism in the New World. It was this that in fact became the source of our heritage. The Congregational Way came first with

[1] Atkins and Fagley, *History of American Congregationalism*, p. 60, quoted from William Bradford.
[2] Ibid: quote from Winslow.

those pilgrim separatists to Plymouth. Then, when a few years later the flood tide of English Puritanism flowed toward America and became the Massachusetts Bay Colony, the two streams united and grew into the fellowship of Christians that we know today as the Congregational Churches.

This story, of course, is the story only of a beginning: the beginning of a movement that has reached to both ends of America, and has become strong in Britain and her Commonwealth countries as well. As the years have passed, and the numbers have grown, changes have come. Life in the nineteenth and twentieth centuries has called for closer bonds between congregations, and so associations, conferences, a General Council, missionary boards, annuity funds, and permanent secretaries came into being. But despite all the changes and all the years, it is still to those first adventurers of the faith that we must turn to find the truest meaning and purpose—the reason for being—of Congregationalism.

One would think that the purpose of a great cause for which even lives were given would not soon be forgotten. And yet Congregationalism is one of the most misunderstood forms of Christian fellowship in the whole of Christ's Church. The tragedy is that it is misunderstood even by Congregationalists.

We are living today in a period which, for the life of the whole Church, is much like that period of late Reformation in England. For Congregationalism particularly, this is a time of crisis. We stand at an important cross-roads. A new hope is filling Christian hearts. A movement is swelling to heal the divisions in the Christian Church—to make the "body of Christ" whole again. It is a hope and an excitement that all of us share. But we must be ready. The wisdom and understanding of each group within this "body of Christ" must run deep. Each must know what its treasure is, what gift it has to offer. But we Congregationalists have forgotten. We no longer understand what we are.

As so often happens when the years pass and generations come and go, the sense of our unique heritage has dimmed and been reduced to but one simple idea: freedom. We have begun to think that liberty is the sum and substance of Congregationalism's uniqueness. Some call it democracy, but by whatever name it is called, we mean this right of a church to legislate for itself as conscience leads, free from coercion by anyone. This alone we clutch to our bosoms, thinking it is our most priceless treasure.

But look at it! Look at it critically in the churches you know, and in the bright light of everyday life. How often it proves to be an empty treasure, a gift misunderstood and badly used. Freedom is certainly a great part of our uniqueness, but we have forgotten why we were given it, and why some men risked homeland, security, and even life to win it.

Look again across the years to the church at Scrooby. Did they become Congregationalists just because they did not like the form and government of the established church? Not for a minute! Church polity was no sacred thing to them. Their concern was far different from ecclesiastical politics. Their concern was for Christ!

To those men and women the New Testament seemed to be saying that to people who faithfully gathered together with open and asking hearts the Risen Christ would come. They believed that the one thing that made it possible for Him to come to them was their common love for Him;

that it was His presence among them—and this alone— that made them a church. Their only reason for existing as a group, their only reason for separating from the Church of England and suffering persecution, was that they might know the abiding presence of the Living Christ. The Anglican Church believed that that presence depended upon bishops and priests in apostolic succession. Even Presbyterian churches believed a church was not a church without a minister.

But those Separatists knew the promise of the Scriptures, and were ready to die to make their point. If Christ promised to be present to ordinary simple believers, then that was the kind of church they were determined to be. How could they acknowledge two rulers of the Church? Christ was their only authority—not the queen and not the bishops and not the ministers. And yet some of them were hung for saying it was so.

The reason they wanted to be free was so that no canon laws, no disciplines, nor any state edicts could ever take the place of Christ—ever keep Him away from His Church. They were not anarchists. They did not want freedom for its own sake. It was so they could be free to obey only Christ that they sought freedom.

But never forget that they saw themselves as obligated to a real obedience: a much higher and harder obedience than that of a church that depends upon rules and orders. Freedom was their treasure because only in freedom could they be fully open to hear the Word that their Lord was speaking in their midst.

Those Englishmen, our forefathers, did not claim freedom from God's Word, but *for* that Word. It was only that they might submit themselves to this higher obedience that they claimed the right to be free. Indeed, if it could be proven that an episcopal or other form of church life could better serve the Gospel; could more effectively foster the spiritual freedom and brotherhood of the conscience that only the Gospel creates; then our free Congregational churches would have no right or reason to exist.

The polity and structural organization in itself meant little to the Pilgrims. The Gospel meant everything. I believe it is at this point that we American Congregationalists have betrayed our heritage. For too many of us—our concern for church liberty has become a political concern. We have stood for freedom not so that Christ could tell us what to do, but so that *no* one could tell us what to do. When spiritual and evangelical liberty become substituted by this rational and political liberty, then the driving force, the enthusiasm and motivation of free churches soon dies.

When this has happened to a congregational church it forfeits its claim to being a truly New Testament Church. Such a church may be a kind of club, or fraternity, but not a church. And I do not mean churches that are remote and distant. I do not mean somebody else's church. Every Congregational church you know is in danger of this perversion.

The danger can be averted only by a deeper understanding on the part of every Congregational layman both of his church and of his Lord. We have been in the habit of regarding ourselves as "low church," and groups like the Episcopalians as "high church." And yet in a real sense, we are the ones with a "high" doctrine of the Church. We have a higher view of the way Christ makes Himself known to His Church—a view that demands a higher responsibility from each member. It is a responsibility to love Christ Jesus and serve Him without the help of ecclesiastical authority and canon law; a responsibility to read the Bible, to pray, to give, to worship, and to work as a result of the discipline that Christ Himself imposes upon us.

These things are said here because I believe that a Congregational church at its best is a fellowship in which Christ can speak and act with a special power. And it is said because there do not seem to be among us enough Congregational churches that are living at their best.

Through those courageous and deeply committed Christians who worshipped at Scrooby Manor, and then set forth for an unknown land with only Christ as their guide—through those "Pilgrim Fathers" of the Congregational Way in America—our Lord has given us a heritage beyond any price.

This book is written out of a conviction that for many of us this heritage has become the forgotten heritage. In seventeenth century England Christ gave us a great destiny. With all my heart I believe it is our destiny still.

1. The Saints at Savoy

I. The Beginnings of the Congregational Way

1. *Congregationalists in England*

For most of us American Congregationalists our history has become a rather vague thing. Plymouth Rock we know —and the Pilgrims. The story of their brave venture across the wild Atlantic to the barren coasts of New England is one of the romances of America that is safe in the storehouse of our treasured memories. Some even remember Scrooby Manor, the trip to Leyden, and the Bradfords, and Brewsters, and Robinsons who made that story live. And they came, something tells us, in the cause of freedom.

But what more do we recall? The founding of Harvard College? The halfway covenant? The Salem witch-trials? Jonathan Edwards? The Unitarian split? For most of us, not even these.

And yet today there is a hunger among us to know who we are, to understand our principles, to make our witness in the Christian world. Quite rightly, we want an end to vagueness. We look for an anchor: some event, some document, some principle that will help us to say, "Look, this is what we are, here is where we stand, this is the rock from which we are hewn!"

In the course of this search, some of us, young pastors and laymen alike, have discovered the English Congregationalists. Not those who came in 1620 to Plymouth, but the English Congregationalists of today: the men and women who are descended from those separatists who never left their native land. And we have found them to be living strangely, in a tradition quite different from ours. Their concerns are different. Their spirit is different. Their aim is different.

Many things were gained when Congregationalism came to America. But some things were lost. Some things were lost to America which have lived on in Britain and are there today to be recovered. It is in England one suspects, that the strongest anchors of world Congregationalism are still wedged firm and sure. Partly because they have had to hold hard to their witness in opposition to a State church.

For this reason it seems legitimate for a book like this to turn to a document written in the year 1658 in the city of London, England to find the touch-stone for its point of view in answering the question, "What is the Congregational Way?". The document is called the Savoy Platform, and it was written by a group of Congregational ministers gathered at London's Savoy Palace to give written expression for the first time to what they conceived to be the Congregational Way which they had been living and evolving for more than a century.

The decades previous had been times of such political and religious crisis that the writing of such a document had become a crucial necessity. It is to the mounting events of these decades and the background they provide that we must now turn.

2. *Elizabeth and the Reformation*

It was Elizabeth who in the last twenty-five years of the sixteenth century finally drove Catholicism from power in England. In a sense the Reformation was secure. And yet, at the beginning of her reign, she was faced with a number of difficulties.

Under Mary the Church and its clergy had been largely Roman Catholic. For this reason, in her religious settlement, Elizabeth allowed the Church, both in its officials and in its worship, to be patterned, as far as her Protestant subjects would allow, after the older Catholic worship. Most of the former Roman clergy conformed to this modified Protestantism and the few who did not were permitted to remain quietly in their parishes.

But this was not the whole story. A fervent popular religious life was growing and spreading in the England of Elizabeth, where there had been only apathy under Henry VIII, Edward VI and Mary. Moreover, men who had been banished under Mary were returning from Geneva and Zürich deeply influenced by the more radical Protestantism of those lands, and bringing with them an aggressiveness that was not to take easily the compromises of Elizabeth. They saw elements of Roman superstition still in English worship and were determined to do away with such hold-overs as prescribed clerical dress, kneeling at the Lord's Supper, and the making of the sign of the cross at Baptism. Because they wanted to purify the church, the men of this party became known as the "Puritans."

Beginning with the controversy over clerical vestments in

1566, repressive measures were employed by which a number of Puritan ministers were driven from their pulpits. This only caused the Puritans to search their Bibles the more carefully to see if an ecclesiastical system which behaved with such unscriptural lovelessness could possibly be intended by God. Furthermore, John Calvin's influence from Geneva convinced them that the Bible held a form of church government quite different from the English form—one in which discipline was in the hands of local elders, in which ministers received office by consent of the congregation, and in which all those who held spiritual office were essentially equal. This was Presbyterianism and the radical Puritans began to move in this direction.

These Presbyterian Puritans hoped to inject as much Puritan practice and discipline into the English church as they could and wait for the government to complete this reformation. They were opposed to all separation from the Church of England. But gradually there began to appear groups of Puritans who were ready to "tarry for none." They were unwilling to wait for a generation or more to pass, but wanted to see the church reformed immediately and were prepared to go even to the lengths of separation to bring it to pass. These were called "Separatists," and were the first to live according to the "Congregational Way."

To them the only Church was a local group of believers in Christ gathered together and united to Him and to each other by a voluntary covenant. Their vision was of Christ as head of each such church, with no church having authority over another, but each owing the other brotherly help and affection.

But in 1583 articles were passed which forbade all private

religious meetings, as well as requiring use of the Prayer Book and of prescribed clerical dress, and from that time on Puritans and Separatists alike were subject to ever increasing repression under the heavy hand of Elizabeth and her bishops.

The screws were being tightened on the Puritans and Separatists for rather natural reasons. With these dissenting groups claiming Divine authority for their ecclesiastical systems, it could have been expected that the high church party would begin to do the same. Until 1604, the Archbishop of Canterbury had been a man who had favored episcopacy more because of its reasonableness than because of any great Scriptural support. But with the accession of Richard Bancroft in that year, and even during the few years previous, a real movement grew among the Anglicans to claim a Divine right for their system.

By 1592 the court of the High Commission had become a most effective weapon against the dissenters. It was a special court not bound by ordinary legal procedure, which was set up by the government to deal with ecclesiastical affairs. A man was presumed guilty when accused and the nature of the proof needed to convict was never clearly defined. It had power anywhere in England to examine and imprison, and it became the primary weapon for enforcing obedience to episcopal authority.

On March 24th, 1603 Elizabeth's reign ended with these problems of authority and discipline still in turmoil.

3. *James I, a Period of Further Oppression*

Following the death of Elizabeth, James I, the son of Mary "Queen of Scots," became King. It was under him that in 1611 our "authorized" or King James version of the

Bible was written. This was the only reform the Puritans got. They were ordered to conform to the episcopal way and in 1604 many of the practices which had offended the Puritans were enacted into law.

It was during these years of growing oppression that Separatist congregations like the one at Scrooby were formed and, after attempting to exist in England, finally chose voluntarily to exile themselves to Leyden in order to worship freely and in safety. Later, in 1620, a minority of that Leyden Congregational Church sailed in the Mayflower across the Atlantic to plant Congregationalism in the New World.

In England, in the meantime, Puritanism was growing in strength, and all through the reign of James was increasing in effectiveness as a political force. When James openly flouted the Puritan concern for a strict Sabbath by urging the return of popular games and dances on Sundays, he quite naturally aroused Puritan ire. But this was not all. At the same time, he was treating Parliament with an unlawful arbitrariness, was giving no real support to German Protestants in the Thirty Years War, and was trying to arrange marriage with a Spanish princess for his heir. All this was resented by his people, and soon even the political sympathies of the House of Commons were leaning more and more toward the Puritans. At the same time James was forcing a royally controlled episcopacy on the self-governing freedom of Scottish Presbyterianism. By the time his reign ended in 1625, there were serious rumblings of religious and political discontent in both England and Scotland.

4. *Charles I and the Oppression under Bishop Laud*

With the death of James and the accession of his son Charles I, events moved rapidly toward a situation of crisis. It was under Charles that William Laud was made Archbishop of Canterbury, bringing in the period of greatest oppression of the Puritans. He was bitterly opposed to Calvinism and although no Roman Catholic, Laud was imperious and arbitrary in his high-church demand for conformity. The House of Commons was Calvinist in its sympathies and politically was increasingly resentful of Charles' frequently arbitrary imposition of taxes without their consent. The rift between Parliament and King grew so wide that in 1629 Charles decided to rule without Parliament. The Anglican party made the serious mistake of allowing itself to be identified with these actions of the King.

It was soon after this that many of the Puritans protested by emigrating to America. By 1640 probably 20,000 of these people had crossed the Atlantic to Massachusetts. They were not Separatists. They were ministers and men of the established church, but they looked for freedom, and they took the Bible as their guide in matters of church organization. Thus it was that the churches they founded in Massachusetts Bay were, like those of their Separatist compatriots in Plymouth, congregational in form.

Storm clouds had been gathering all over Britain and it was in Scotland that they finally broke and poured down their wrath upon Charles' head. Presbyterianism in Scotland had been defeated primarily by James I's granting church lands to the nobles and thereby winning their support. But Charles, at the beginning of his reign, quite justly returned these lands to the church, thereby pushing these nobles into sympathy with the aggrieved and persecuted Presbyterians. From that point on, the two groups began to make common cause against the episcopally-controlled church and the royal power that stood behind it.

Wanting religious uniformity, Charles in 1637, at the instigation of Archbishop Laud, ordered all the Scottish Churches to use a liturgy practically identical to the Church of England liturgy. Edinburgh rioted when it was used in that city on July 23rd. Scotland flamed into open rebellion. A National Covenant was drawn up in February of 1638 and was signed by thousands. In December the Scottish General Assembly deposed the bishops and rejected the whole ecclesiastical system that had been chafing and persecuting them since 1597. This was war, and thus began that romantic and daring chapter in Scotland's religious history which all of us know as the age of the Covenanters.

Charles raised troops to fight the Scots and in order to pay the costs of war was finally forced to call Parliament back into session in 1640. After dissolving the 1640 Parliament, events forced him from one bad move to another. Being invaded by the Scots and being forced to come to terms with them, Charles found that he had no choice but to call Parliament back again.

This time Presbyterian Puritanism was in control. Archbishop Laud was imprisoned. The High Commission, with its frightening record of persecution, was abolished. In 1642, the King accused five members of Parliament of treason and tried to arrest them. Civil War broke out across the realm and soon Parliament and its Puritan armies were embattled against the King and his troops.

5. *Civil War and the Restoration of Religious Liberties*

It was in 1643 during these early stages of England's great Civil War that Parliament then determined that a new creed and government of the church must be agreed upon. Therefore, it invited to Westminster an assembly of one hundred and twenty-one ministers and thirty laymen to give its advice on the new church polity. The great majority of these were Presbyterians, who, together with a handful of Congregationalists and Episcopalians, formed the famous Westminster Assembly.

The Scots, whose help had been sought by Parliament in the War, carried tremendous influence in the Assembly. The final results of its recommendation was that a Directory of Worship, containing an avowedly Presbyterian form of Church government, and the famous Westminster Confession was established by Parliament in 1646, and 1648 respectively. Also in 1648 both a Larger and Shorter Catechism were approved. These are the great documents of Presbyterianism that are still the spiritual and ecclesiastical guideposts for Presbyterians both in Scotland and in America.

During this period a significant change took place in the status of Congregationalism in England. Ten or eleven of the members of this Westminster Assembly were Congregationalists. Several of them had been persecuted under Archbishop Laud, had fled to Holland and ministered to Congregations there, and were now again in England in positions of responsibility. They were in agreement with the Presbyterians on matters of doctrine. Their difference was one of polity and their great concern was that in the new religious laws there would be not only a place in the sun for Presbyterianism, but a real tolerance for the smaller religious groups as well.

Their minute number in the Assembly would never have given them much of a hearing except for one interesting and increasingly important factor. The fortunes of the War itself were causing a spread of Independency, as Congregationalism was and still is called in England, all over the country. In 1644 the royal army had been badly beaten on Marston Moor by the parliamentary army of Oliver Cromwell. Less than a year later Cromwell practically destroyed the King's army near Naseby. Charles himself became a captive of the English Parliament, and the prestige of Cromwell and his volunteer army soared.

This army was actually a crew of religious enthusiasts who were bitterly opposed to Rome and everything smacking of Romanism, and who were of a distinctly independent point-of-view. These men were as much opposed to the rigid Presbyterianism in Parliament as they had been to the authority of Bishops. Cromwell shared this view and was widely known to lean in sympathy toward Congregationalism.

The Presbyterian majority in the Westminster Assembly realized therefore that these few Congregationalists represented a growing power both in Parliament and the nation and for that reason gave them a greater hearing. The Congregationalists, for their part, voiced opposition and caused considerable delay in the acceptance of the Presbyterian forms of church government for the same reason—they knew their own power was increasing.

The Congregationalists were somewhat loath to present a definite alternative plan of their own for fear of losing the support of an army made up of a diverse assortment of religious viewpoints. It was probably this weakness that allowed the Presbyterians to influence Parliamentary enactment of various Presbyterian laws and creeds.

However, radical changes came within a few years. The army rose to real control in England, the Scots fell away and were defeated in a second civil war. Presbyterians were more and more expelled from Parliament, the king was executed, the Commonwealth under the Protectorate of Cromwell was established, and a new day of tolerance and influence was ushered in for Congregationalists.

With their numbers growing and their ministers respected and in more influential positions, these Congregationalists felt the need of having their doctrinal and ecclesiastical position more clearly defined.

6. *Preparation for Savoy*

Up to this point there had been in England no Congregational denomination as such; no fellowship of churches and ministers with common point-of-view, common concerns, or a commonly declared conviction of faith. Rejecting both Presbyterian and Episcopal tests of faith and worship, they wanted nevertheless to give testimony to the faith they did share. They wanted no close-bound ecclesiastical structure, but they did want to share as churches in the fellowship of Christian brothers who were walking in a common Way.

It was out of this sense of need that with the personal, but not official approval of Cromwell and the State, a letter went out on June 21, 1658 from a Mr. Griffiths in the name "of the congregational elders in and about London" inviting leading Congregational ministers in the several counties to call the churches of the Congregational Way in their neighborhoods to be present by pastor or delegate at an Assembly at the Savoy Palace, London, on the 29th of the following September.

The death of Cromwell before the assembly was able to convene, made void its work as far as any future establishment of Congregationalism. And yet this meeting of the Congregational "saints" at Savoy did mark the actual beginning of a defined Congregational Way in England and laid foundations of a pure Congregationalism for which all generations to come might be thankful. Leaving now the course of history which led to the Savoy, let us look for a moment at what this Assembly said to its time and to our time.[2]

II. THE SAVOY DECLARATION

1. *Preface*

The Savoy Declaration is divided into two sections: a Confession of Faith, and a Platform of Polity. Although it has been called long and dreary, one of the most fascinating features of the Declaration for Americans today is the Preface which accompanied it.

Its words may have had a familiar ring to the seventeenth century Englishmen who bought the first copies at John Allen's book shop in London, during 1658, but it bespeaks a concern long lost on the ears of modern American Congregationalists. Running as a now swelling, now modulated theme throughout the Preface is a note strange to us: the

[2] The material for this historical section has been drawn from Williston Walker's *History of the Christian Church*, pp. 457-473, and also his *Creeds and Platforms of Congregationalism*, pp. 342-348.

continued and oft-repeated concern for the "Spirit of Christ."

The Preface speaks with some eloquence of the unanimity of the Savoy meeting and of its Congregational concern for freedom and tolerance. Because these ideas are familiar, it would be easy for us today to see nothing more than these features in the Preface. After all, freedom is a watchword with us modern-day Independents, and our times are all too congenial to unanimity. But even when the Preface is expounding these ideas, it seems to be doing so in the light of a much deeper concern and passion: the "Spirit of Christ."

Whether the writer is talking of how amazing it was that the delegates got along so well together and could agree so readily, or whether it is his plea for more freedom and greater tolerance for the Independent churches of the realm, always there is this sense of "the Spirit" that seems to be undergirding and supporting his arguments.

In introducing the Confession, the theme of the Preface is that when confessions are made by a group of believing Christians together, it is a demonstration of the oneness of their faith, of the way in which they are "perfectly joined in the same minde." The very willingness with which people assent to such a confession, it says, gives beauty to the confession itself. The Spirit of Christ is a free and gentle Spirit that gently leads men into all truth, and so a natural characteristic of His people is the willingness to be led by Him. Already the great foundation of Congregationalism is being laid.

The whole concern of the Preface was to tell the world that these Congregational "Saints at Savoy" have been led by the Spirit. The temper of the times is the first proof given. Because it had been a time full of so many contrary winds of doctrine, these Congregational fathers had had to think through their faith very carefully. There they were, meeting at the Savoy, and attesting in one body to all the great truths of the faith in Holy Scripture. "What is this," cries the writer, "but tryed Faith indeed? And equivalent to a new conversion into the truth? An anchor that is proved to be sure and steadfast, that will certainly hold in all contrary storms . . ." [3] The fact that all these independent Congregationalists had, like the converts of the Apostles, stood fast in the truth in spite of all the temptations to stray, was "in itself as great a work and instance of the power of God . . ." [4] Up to this point they had been nothing but hundreds of separate churches setting the same course and living by the same convictions in a terribly difficult time without any help from each other. And yet still they had held strong and not compromised their stand.

A second proof the writer finds is the fact that the Savoy Assembly makes such a prominent principle of the freedom of Christians of all persuasions—even those of questionable orthodoxy—"to enjoy all ordinances and spiritual privileges according to their light, as freely as any other of their brethren that pretend to the greatest orthodoxy." [5] For even while they insisted on "This just liberty of Saints in all the Churches of Christ, we ourselves have had no need of it" because God had mercifully kept their own orthodoxy above question. Thus they say in the words of the Apostles, "we have stood fast in the liberty wherewith Christ hath

---

[3] Walker, *Creeds and Platforms,* p. 357.
[4] Ibid.
[5] Ibid.

made us free . . ." [6] Again, it is Christ Who has kept them true to their principles.

The fact that it took such a short time to agree on its declaration, stands with the writer of the Preface as an added proof of the power of Christ's Spirit among them. "It is therefore to be looked at as a great and special work of the Holy Ghost that so numerous a company . . . should so readily, speedily, and joyntly give up themselves unto such a whole Body of Truth . . ." [7]

The conclusion he voices for the whole Assembly is that "this is no other than the Lord's doing." [8] The repeated theme again and again is that the Spirit of Christ has led them; that He is the One Who gives them power and authority as churches; and that nothing else is needed—only God in the midst of His people.

> ". . . So the Saints when not abiding scattered, but gathered under their respective Pastors according to God's heart unto an house . . . such together are . . . the most steady and firm pillar and seat of Truth that God hath anywhere appointed unto Himself on earth, where His truth is best conserved, and publiquely held forth . . ." [9]

Their Lord is the charter of their church. He is the foundation of their Way. And so the real essence of Congregationalism emerges.

The rest of the Preface is simply an amplification and justification of this old, yet new, free, and exciting form of Church polity. It is made abundantly clear that their faith and their doctrine is essentially the same as that of

[6] Op. Cit., p. 358.
[7] Op. Cit., p. 359.
[8] Ibid.
[9] Op. Cit., p. 360.

the Presbyterians. The difference is in polity, and this Preface hesitates not for a minute to testify to the Congregationalist's conviction that the Congregational Way is Christ's Way—clearly set forth in Scripture, long before episcopacy or Presbyterianism were even thought of. "What we have laid down and asserted about CHURCHES and their government, we humbly conceive to be the order which Christ Himself hath ordered to be observed, (and) we have endeavored to follow Scripture-light . . ." [10]

It is in this overpowering sense of Christ's leading, and of being a peculiar people charged to live out a bold experiment, that the Saints at Savoy present their Declaration to the world.

2. Confession of Faith

Although the Confession of Faith was the section of the Savoy Declaration that most influenced American Congregationalism, of the two parts it was the less original. The Preface hammered home the point that these Congregationalists, different as they might be in polity, were in matters of faith orthodox to the core. Let their Presbyterian brethren make no mistake about this, the Congregationalists were with them in doctrine.

Both groups were deeply influenced by the continental Reformers and they shared at many points the sometimes rather dogmatic Calvinism that, from Geneva, was influencing all the reformed churches. To prove it, the saints at Savoy used, with the exception of one or two whole sections and a number of minor changes, the Confession written at Westminster by the Presbyterians as their own. On the

[10] Op. Cit., p. 364.

great fundamentals of the faith they were at one with the whole reformation movement.

Above all, their faith was rooted and grounded in Scripture. The Bible, interpreted by the Holy Spirit, they took to be their sole guide in faith. And they were Trinitarian, believing God to be known in Three Persons: Father, Son, and Holy Ghost. "Which doctrine of the Trinity is the foundation of all our communion with God, and comfortable Dependence upon Him . . ." [11] which indeed, the rest of the Confession bears out.

In some of it there breathes a warm evangelical fire, in other parts an arbitrary dogmatism which most of us would want today to see tempered by love. Nearly every conceivable question of faith is answered, from the role of civil magistrates to the question of the Last Judgment. It is thorough, methodical, and in many ways the same as would have been attested by any Presbyterians of the day.

It came, in fact, to be used extensively in New England through Connecticut's later Saybrook Platform. Curiously, the Savoy Assembly's really original work, the section on Congregational polity, found little hearing in the New World. It is this section and its implications, however, that today can be most helpful to American Congregational churchmen.

3. *Polity in England and America*

One of the sorrows of Congregationalism in America is that it became so quickly embroiled in matters of discipline and detail. In a new world, with houses to be built, schools to be established, food to be raised, and a whole new life

[11] Op. Cit., p. 370, the Savoy Declaration.

to be won from the wilderness, it is not surprising that in communities in which the civil government and the church were practically identical that church was forced to face tensions and decisions that under ordinary conditions no church would ever have to face.

To those of us twentieth century churchmen who occasionally have to keep peace over questions of decor and dimension in our modern building projects, imagine the fortitude of our fathers who had to decide together even personal matters of whose house was to be built where, how the corn should be planted, how provisions should be divided, and who should go to treat with Chief Massasoit and his braves! Wonder of wonders that they stayed together at all!

But to live together did mean a perhaps undue emphasis on church discipline. The brethren were more aware of each other's failings. Like some of us in New England still, they knew more about one another than was good for them. Witch-trials and "Half-Way Covenants" were the more obvious and tragic results.

Perhaps less obvious but more pervasive was the tendency toward rigidity, and authoritarianism, and legalism in point-of-view that was fostered.

This meant that Congregationalism in New England was not left to grow quite so freely and openly as the Congregationalism of old England. The institution of the Church Meeting, that instrument of brotherly love and understanding so important to England, was in America later lost to the town meeting, since both were serving the same people and covering many of the same concerns. That the freer meeting dedicated to the Will of God was the one dropped, has been to our subsequent impoverishment.

In this and many other features American Congregationalism *had* to be definite, legal, and authoritative at an
earlier age. Thus, the Savoy Platform of Polity presents us
with the broad outline of a new way of church life not yet
rigidly defined, but still full and sweeping and open to
development.

The two or three pages of its points underline several
important convictions these Congregationalists had about
what a Christian church should be and about how the
Christian life and faith of its people should be lived. It is
out of some of these concerns that the chapters of this
book have grown. Suffice it now that we mention these
great convictions and comment briefly in passing on their
significance.

4. *Polity of the Savoy Platform*

The Assembly at Savoy saw as the first great principle of
church government the sovereignty or headship of Christ—
Christ alone the power in the Church, Christ the ruler of
each congregation.

> "By the appointment of the Father all Power for the Calling.
> Institution, Order or Government of the Church is invested
> in a Supreme and Soveraign maner in the Lord Jesus Christ,
> as King and Head thereof." [12]

The next great principle was the idea of the Gathered
Church—not the Church as a hierarchical institution com-
prising many congregations; not the Church as individual
congregations called into being by ecclesiastical fiat of pope,
or bishop, or even of council; and certainly not the Church
simply by virtue of the presence in its midst of a properly

---

[12] Op. Cit., p. 403, the Savoy Declaration, Article I.

ordained priest or pastor. What they meant was the Church made up of individual Christians in a given geographical place gathered together by Christ through their common love for Him.

". . . the Lord Jesus calleth out on the World unto Communion with himself, those that are given unto him by his Father, that they may walk before him in all the ways of obedience . . .

Those thus called . . . he commandeth to walk together in particular societies or churches . . ." [13]

These saints at Savoy were convinced also that God's Word in the Bible was the only authority the church needed for the testing of its faith and for the common discipline of its life. Episcopalians could have their *Book of Common Prayer* and the Presbyterians their *Book of Order*. But as for Congregationalists the *Bible* would be their book.

"To each of these Churches thus gathered, according unto his minde declared in his Word, he hath given all that Power and Authority, which is in any way needfull for their carrying on that Order in Worship and Discipline, which he hath instituted for them to observe . . ." [14]

In order for Christians to walk together in the freedom of this higher kind of discipline the Savoy divines knew that they must live under some common agreement among themselves, and between themselves and Christ. Thus they appropriated for Congregationalism the great Christian doctrine of the Covenant relationship—the relationship of men bound together not by law, but freely in the mutual

[13] Ibid, from Articles II & III.
[14] Ibid, from Article IV.

agreement of love—and enthroned it at the very heart of their Congregational Way.[15]

> "The Members of these Churches are Saints by Calling . . . (and) . . . do willingly consent to walk together according to the appointment of Christ, giving up themselves unto the Lord, and to one another by the will of God in professed subjection to the Ordinances of the Gospel." [16]

The conviction of the Savoy Assembly was that, since Christ had given full ecclesiastical and spiritual power to individual gathered churches of Christian people, the calling of a minister or any other officers into the service of such a church was the prerogative and privilege not of a bishop, nor of a presbytery, but of the members of the church themselves. Therefore they laid it down that the Congregational Way of calling a minister should be by election by all the people. They implied also that even the ordination and installation of a minister was properly to be done by the church through the power vested in it by Christ.

> "The way appointed by Christ for the calling of any person, fitted and gifted by the holy Ghost, unto the office of Pastor, Teacher or Elder in a Church, is, that he be chosen thereunto by the common suffrage of the Church itself, and solemnly set apart by fasting and Prayer, with Imposition of Hands of the Eldership of that Church, if there be any before constituted therein . . .
>
> "The essence of this Call of a Pastor . . . unto Office, consists in the Election of the Church, together with his acceptation of it, and separation by Fasting and Prayer . . ." [17]

[15] The idea of the "Covenant" has been very important in Presbyterianism as well; but there it is a covenant theology of a whole Church denomination—a rather different thing from the Congregational use of the covenant as the direct and binding authority of each local church.
[16] Walker, *Creeds and Platforms*, p. 404, from Article VIII.
[17] Op. Cit., pp. 404-405, from Articles XI & XII.

In a way of Church life so essentially a *layman's* church, in which the people themselves are of tremendous importance, it seemed right and fitting to those early Congregationalists at Savoy to insure that the preaching of the Word would not be confined to any priestly class but would be accepted as the free gift of God to whomever He should choose to give it. So another great Congregational practice, that of lay preaching, was given its foundation at Savoy.

"Although it be incumbent on the Pastors and Teachers of the Churches to be instant in Preaching the Word, by way of Office; yet the work of Preaching the Word is not so peculiarly confined to them, but that others also gifted and fitted by the holy Ghost for it . . . may publiquely, ordinarily, and constantly perform it." [18]

Moreover, it seemed to them a special necessity of the Congregational Way that the ministry be not only of a preaching, but also of a pastoral nature—and that pastoral relationship an evangelical one, too! If Congregationalism was to be a way of the people, then those people must be bound together in a very concrete way by the constant and faithful care of a loving pastor going in and out among them.

"However, they who are ingaged in the work of Publique Preaching . . . ought . . . not to neglect others living within their Parochial Bounds, but besides their constant Publique Preaching to them, they ought to enquire after their profiting by the Word, instructing them in, and pressing upon them . . . the great Doctrines of the gospel, even personally and particularly, so far as their strength and time will admit." [19]

[18] Op. Cit., p. 405, from Article XIII.
[19] Ibid., from Article XIV.

The principle of Congregational authority demanded, as far as Savoy was concerned, not only that Pastors should be elected to office by the Church, but that each member should be elected to office by the other members—again exalting the principle of Christ's authority in the midst of the gathered church, and emphasizing the freedom and fairness of the Christian's liberty in Christ.

> "In the carrying on of Church-administrations, no person ought to be added to the Church, but by the consent of the Church itself; that so love . . . may be preserved between all the members thereof." [20]

Because the Congregational understanding of the Church found the life of Christians always to be within the fellowship of particular congregations, they held with no foolishness about Christians having church membership in wider groupings known as dioceses or presbyteries, or about being called Christians without membership in *some* local church. Nor could they grant to any such groups authority to censure or discipline ministers or members in local churches, or local churches themselves.

> "As all Believers are bound to join themselves to particular Churches, when and where they have opportunity to do so . . .
>
> The power of Censures being seated by Christ in a particular Church, is to be exercised only towards particular Members of each Church respectively as such; and there is no power given by him unto any Synods or Ecclesiastical Assemblies to Excommunicate, or to . . . threaten . . . other church—censures against Churches, Magistrates, or their people on any account . . ." [21]

[20] Ibid., from Article XVII.
[21] Op. Cit., p. 406, from Articles XX & XXII.

For these early Congregationalists it was vitally important to establish beyond doubt that the real life of the Church was in the geographical particularity of local gathered congregations of Christ's people. But having done that they were quick to testify to the reality of Christian fellowship among these many churches of the Congregational Way. Indeed, as the Statement of Faith reiterates over and over again, they felt an obligation to love and work with churches not of the Congregational Way, but who were of sound doctrine, loving the Lord Jesus. They were perfectly happy to work with their Presbyterian brethren for instance, and always made the point that they shared with them an orthodoxy of faith. And so they laid down as a principle of Congregationalism the obligation of Christians and their churches to love, pray for, and fellowship with churches of Christ everywhere.

> "As all Churches and all Members of them are bound to pray continually for the good or prosperity of all the Churches of Christ in all places . . . So the Churches themselves . . . ought to hold communion amongst themselves for their peace, increase of love, and mutual edification." [22]

Carrying this further, they made plain that there was a place for churches to gather together to consider and give advice on mutual problems. However, they made it even plainer that such councils have no "Church-Power," with jurisdiction over churches or individuals, and that indeed, such occasional advisory councils are the only kind instituted by Christ, and any which subordinate churches in any way are not of Him.

> ". . . It is according to the minde of Christ, that many Churches holding communion together, do by their Mes-

[22] Op. Cit., p. 407, from Article XXV.

sengers meet in a . . . council, to consider and give their advice . . .

"Howbeit these Synods so assembled are not entrusted with any Church-Power . . . or with any Jurisdiction over the Churches themselves . . .

Besides these occasional Synods or Councils, there are not . . . any Synods appointed by Christ in a way of Subordination to one another." [23]

And finally, in the same irenic spirit of the whole Savoy meeting, these Congregational saints proclaim to the world the great Congregational and Christian principle of the freedom of the Lord's Table. All Christians who love the Lord Jesus and are trying sincerely to live the life of Christian faith are to be made welcome at the Sacrament of the Lord's Supper even though they be of another "Way" than the Congregational. One of the sins of the Church is that this principle of Christian freedom and love so clearly set forth in 1658 and a cardinal tenet of Congregationalism through all the intervening years, has yet—even three hundred years later—to be accepted by some of the most important Christian Communions of our world today.

Here the spirit of their declaration:

"Such reforming Churches as consist of Persons sound in the Faith and of Conversation becoming the Gospel, ought not to refuse the Communion of each other, so far as may consist with their own Principles respectively, though they walk not in all things according to the same Rules of Church-Order." [24]

So the Saints at Savoy established the basis of a Way of Church-life which they believed to be radically new and yet as old as the Faith itself. They called it Congregational,

[23] Ibid., from Articles XXVI & XXVII.
[24] Op. Cit., p. 408, from Article XXIX.

but they believed in their hearts that it was Christian, *the* Christian Way. They were not dogmatic in this belief. They simply felt, with the confidence of one who treasures a great secret within, that this was the way their Christ meant His people to live. They believed that His way was always meant to be the way of the gathered community, knowing, and loving, and sharing with one another in such freedom and depth that there—above all other places—the Spirit of Christ could be present in power to make Himself known to His people.

It was a grand vision, the master-strokes of a way of life whose relevance for Christian people is perhaps greater today than it was at Savoy, three centuries ago. For there is a hunger among Christians today to find a common ground, a way of church life they can share—for all their differences—as one people.

Some, even in Congregationalism, have been searching in Episcopacy for that ground. And yet here, in the rare combination of freedom within the higher discipline of obedience to the Holy Spirit, is a way in which all Christians could walk.

It is out of this conviction regarding the ecumenical Church and out of this vision of a new way of Church-life seen by the Saints at Savoy that the succeeding chapters of this book have grown.

2. The Way of the Covenant People

Having followed the lines of history through the early days of our denomination and having inquired into the concerns of a group of Congregationalists of another land and another time, come with me now back to America, back to the mid-twentieth century, and back to our own cities and villages, and to our own churches.

Savoy is all right. They knew what they thought about Congregationalism. They had fashioned their ideas under the pressure of persecution and tempered them in the heat of controversy. They stood on solid ground, and could answer to any man for their faith.

But what about us? Where do we stand? We call ourselves Congregationalists. Some of us indeed, have been Congregationalists all our lives. But how much do we know about it?

About other ways of church life we have some idea. After the thousands of words and the great splashes of pictures in the public press on the demise of Pius XII and the accession of John XXIII we all know at least that

Rome has a pope and a college of cardinals. We are aware that the Quakers stand for peace. We know that the Episcopalians have a tradition of a rich sacramentalism and an apostolic succession of bishops, that the Methodists proclaim the fervor of an evangelical gospel and a puritan moralism, and that the Baptists believe only adults should be baptized, and that by immersion. Somehow, we seem to know the unique feature in most of the great denominations around us.

But what is the Congregational way? What do we stand for? If you had to do it, what would you name as the one unique feature in the life of your local church and the other Congregational churches you know?

Most of us would stand flat-footed, red-faced, and without an answer. Were we pressed so hard that we had to answer, some of us would probably retort: "Well, we're the *free* church. We are the church with no ecclesiastical controls, no bishops to tell us what to do, just local churches ordering our own affairs and doing and believing what we think right."

These are the catch-words we often hear, and of course, they are part of the answer. But these are days not at all congenial to free churchmanship. Congregationalism even at its best is on the defensive, and to our friends of other persuasions this might sound suspiciously like anarchy. "You can't call that a church!" they say. "You need order, discipline, authority. How can you maintain any standards of church life and membership in an organization as loose as that? No, a handful of people in a local congregation are not enough to make a church!"

And truthfully, we wonder about this ourselves. Freedom is the word we have always heard about Congregationalism.

And yet for thousands in our generation of Congregationalists it has left a sense of vagueness. We do feel somehow as if we are part of a happy anarchy. "We are free, free!" we cry, "no one can tell us what to do!" But when we are pressed to give an accounting of ourselves, we search about for something to put our finger on, for a spot of solid ground on which to stand, and our "way" seems to be wanting.

And yet something within American Congregationalists today seems to be telling them that there must be something more. Congregationalists are reading their history as never before. Denominational executives are searching the past, scanning the future, and offering new interpretations of who we are and what our purpose is. And Congregational people everywhere, like the people of my village church, are wanting to know, seeking answers, and asking again and again, "What does it mean to be a Congregationalist? What should we stand for? How are we supposed to be different?"

There is probably not a Congregational minister today who has not had the experience of a parishioner being honest enough to say "I grew up a Congregationalist, and I still don't know what it's all about. My faith is too vague. I want to know what I ought to believe as a Congregational Christian!"

People today, especially young people, are asking serious questions of the Church. They want a way of worship and a way of church life that means something, that speaks an encouraging and meaningful word to them in their lives amid the tensions of a world gone mad. They are searching for a faith. What kind of answer is it to say: "We are the free churches. Here you can do and believe as you like."

They are not looking for that. They want a Gospel. They want to know if there is a common belief burning in our hearts—a love for Jesus Christ that can point the way and help them to find God. They want to be part of a community of Christians who care about Christ and care about each other.

Every time we fail to give a real answer for the faith that is in us, every time we show them the sorry picture of a church life that does not seem to understand itself and its own uniqueness and power, the way of the authoritarian churches becomes the more tempting for them. There is something secure and definite in the confessions and creeds, the canon laws and the church orders of some of the other historic forms of church life.

In the Episcopal and Presbyterian forms of church life there is authority, order, and a certain security; the kind which Congregationalism doesn't begin to give; the kind it doesn't even try to give. On a superficial reading of our tradition then, it is possible for these young Congregationalists to feel their feet on shifting sand, to grasp for something ready at hand to cling to and at first to find nothing; to look for authority and answers among us and to find us wanting.

The other churches seem to have an orthodoxy of theology, a sense of authority, and a richness of symbol and form that make their own tradition seem a pale picture by comparison. Their churches are often the bare meeting-houses of New England. Their ministers wear only the simple unassuming black of the geneva gown. Theology in their tradition is frequently a matter of considerable disagreement. And its very freedom makes for wide and perhaps confusing differences of witness and tradition.

The result among many of our Congregational people is this insecure sense of not knowing who they are religiously nor what they believe. It is a feeling also of a weakness, a vagueness of thinking, a lack of order, and a vacillation in theology in their own tradition. There is, therefore, an honest desire among these people for something deeper, for a surer rock to stand on, for a more concrete Christ to proclaim, and for a more certain witness to make to the world.

The tragedy is that too often, and in too many ways, their criticism is justified, and their hunger is too real to be denied. Somehow we have failed to show them the depths and the strengths and the peculiar witness of the Congregational Way.

For in our much-advertised freedom many of us have mistakenly thought that the Congregational Way was for each member to believe what he liked, that it was up to each man to decide what Christ's will was for him, and that our "way" *was* something of an anarchy of the spirit—the religious incarnation of democratic individualism.

Instead of being obedient to Christ's will, we have taken our freedom as warrant not to accept Christ's will or anyone else's if we did not want to do so. Through freedom we have in many respects let go our heritage as Bible-centered churches. Through freedom we have often come to care less than we should for our fellowship with sister churches. Through freedom the fire of the missionary imperative has too often flickered low among us.

And so now, with the tides of modern life running swiftly toward larger and more complex structures and toward ever greater conformity, it is small wonder indeed, that when Congregationalists look about at themselves, they are tempted to go the same way. "Why hold out any longer," some say. "Why not tighten the lines of communication and authority so that we can meet the world more efficiently and powerfully? Perhaps we would be stronger churches and better Christians if we did."

We deserve the criticism. We have asked for the problem that faces us. Because we have not really understood ourselves what is the Congregational Way. The charge against us is lack of discipline, absence of authority, and weakness of theology. Hundreds of voices, from within and without our fellowship are asking, "Is there anything strong, and great, and enduring in the Congregational Way that the whole Church needs and which must not be lost whatever the cost? Is there something here which justifies beyond question Congregationalism's right of existence?"

The answer is a resounding "Yes!" There is depth, and vitality, and power in our way of life. There is, in our way, the highest kind of discipline, the most daring sort of authority, and the most enduring form of strength.

It is part of our heritage. It is there to be recovered. And we ignore it at our peril. Its heart is in the concept of "the Covenant People," and its theological foundation is in the word of Jesus, that "Where two or three are gathered together in My Name, there am I in the midst of them."

If there is any one thing a Congregationalist should know about his denomination it is that we are not a denomination without discipline, that anarchy is not our way, that our strength is that we are a "covenant people."

Many churches, like the Church of Rome, the Anglican

Churches of Britain and America, and the great Reformed Churches of the continent and of Scotland and America, are creedal or confessional churches. The test of faith with them is a man's acceptance of a set definition of Christian faith—his ability honestly to declare with all the members of the church he is entering: "I believe in God the Father Almighty, Maker of heaven and earth; And in Jesus Christ His only Son our Lord; Who was conceived by the Holy Ghost; born of the Virgin Mary; Suffered under Pontius Pilate; Was crucified, dead and buried . . . !"

But the great fact for people of the Congregational Way is that Christ made a covenant with His people.[1] He never said, "Believe these items of theology and you are in!" Not Jesus. His word was "Follow Me. Come walk with Me. Live with Me, trust Me, learn My Way, be My disciple!" It was not theological correctness He was interested in, but personal commitment. What Jesus wanted was willingness to live the new life and to walk in faith with His band of brothers.

The Revised Standard Version of the Bible calls the New Testament the "New Covenant." At His last supper with His disciples Jesus said: "This cup is the *new covenant* in my blood which is shed for you and for many for the remission of sins."

A covenant is an agreement—here, an agreement between God and man, as to how they will live with one another, what they will owe to each other, what their relationship will be. The first covenant, the "Old Covenant"

---

[1] See footnote 15 in Chapter I. The covenant idea is by no means exclusively Congregational. It is part of the whole Christian heritage. But it is the Congregational Way particularly which makes a covenant between a congregation of believers and God the actual political and spiritual basis of the organized life of each individual church.

43

that God made with us, was the one written in faith one star-filled night in Canaan when God called Abraham from his tent and said: "I will establish my covenant between Me and thee, and thy seed after thee, in their generations, for an everlasting covenant, to be a God unto thee, and to thy seed after thee" (Genesis 17:8). It was God's agreement with Israel that He would be her God and that she would be His people.

But the New Testament proclaims from beginning to end that God has made a new covenant with His people. It proclaims that nearly two thousand years ago He split history in one mighty event, coming among us in the person of Jesus Christ to shatter the hard shell of man's heart and to break through into a new relationship with him of love, and trust, and saving faith. God's new covenant with Israel, drawn up at Bethlehem and sealed at Calvary, was a promise that through Jesus He would be with them always in the power of a love that dared to die to save them from themselves. It was a promise that in Christ He had defeated sin and sickness, and despair and death, and that they and all men could be victors with Him, if only they would believe. The promise then, the new agreement, the new covenant, was as simple as this: salvation—by faith.

The great words of the new covenant are these: "Where two or three are gathered together in My Name, there am I in the midst of them!" To Congregationalists this has stood as the one fundamental agreement between Christ and His people—that to those who come together in His Name, though only a handful, He will come and be in their midst with power.

This was all He asked: not for bishops, not for canon laws, not for creeds—but only for believing men. Nothing more would ever be needed for Jesus to be present and real to the people of God. And in the experience of the early Church this was proven again and again. After Calvary it seemed like the end of everything for the disciples. Jesus was gone. Their hopes seemed finished forever: Until the amazing miracle of Easter came and made them remember the promise—remember that they were still partners in a covenant that had not been broken. For, when two or three *did* meet together in His Name, He *was* there. First at Emmaus, then back at the upper room, and later to five hundred of the brethren together. Jesus was alive and real and would never leave them: for now they knew. And this became the tremendous, exciting fact of the New Testament Church: when they met believing—Jesus was there.

This is why Congregationalists have believed that the Covenant is the thing. This is why we have believed that it was this agreement Christ made with us that we must always keep. And this is why we have believed that the important thing was not to have a creed, or a bishop, or a special order of service, but to gather together in faith and to open our hearts to discover, if we could, Christ's will for us.

The covenant relation, it has seemed to us, is the real charter of the Church. The Romans can say that no church is a Church without a Pope at the head and ordained clergy in each congregation. The Anglicans can say that it takes an apostolic succession of bishops and a proper liturgy to have a Church. The Reformed churches can cry for "right belief" and for things done "decently and in order" before they will call a church a Church, but Congregationalists find the Bible saying that Christ alone, in the midst of His people, is enough. That if He is there in the gathered church then nothing else is needed.

Certainly this was all the early Church needed: all they needed to make their sacrament of Baptism and the Lord's Supper a redeeming experience; all they needed to strengthen them to live better lives than they had ever lived before; all they needed to send them out to preach the good news with power. For them Christ was enough.

And so also have those of the Congregational Way believed Him to be enough. This is why we are heard to speak so everlastingly of the "Lordship of Christ." If He is King of kings and Lord of lords, then there is none beside Him. He is *our* King, and *our* Lord. It is to Him and to Him alone that we owe our allegiance and obedience.

For us this means that He is Lord and King in His Church: that, whether in my village church in Williamsburg or in one of the great churches of Boston, or Hartford, or Chicago, or California, He rules. And He rules in a direct way, without need of human intermediaries in the form of popes, or bishops, or presbyters—or even ministers for that matter. He can speak and make His will known directly to the gathered people in the local church, great or small.

It is His presence that gives authority to our order, that gives validity to our sacraments, that exercises discipline, and that keeps our faith true to Him and real in power. And it is the covenant that stands in every Congregational church as a constant reminder that we live in this relationship to Christ.

Since the earliest days of Congregationalism this covenant has actually been a written document, an agreement among the original members of a church and between themselves collectively and Christ, that they would walk together as Christian brothers, following the Master and working with and praying for each other, that "loving and being loved, blessing and being blessed, serving and being served, (they might) be prepared while (they) dwell together on earth for the perfect fellowship of the life everlasting." [2]

At the time when most of our churches were first organized, the covenant was written as a deliberate and conscious agreement between the members of the church and Christ. It is so in my little church, where our revised covenant of 1874 states that we will agree "to be subject to the government of Christ, as exercised in this Church as long as we are members of it." I have often wished that we had, as some New England Congregational churches still have, the names of the charter members signed under the covenant and followed by the names of all the new members who have joined the church in all the generations since. What a great thrill it would be and what an irrevocable reminder of our heritage as Congregationalists, to witness our faith and attest our Christian brotherhood by signing our names and pledging our lives with all the saints of the faith who have gone before!

The great source of discipline and authority in the Congregational Way then, is in our life as a "Covenant People."

But this conception of church order would be doomed to irrelevant idealism if it were simply left here. How are Congregationalists today, the people of all kinds and of all ages and of all denominational backgrounds who are coming now into our churches, ever to understand this heritage

[2] From *A Book of Worship for Free Churches*, Oxford Press, New York. 1950, p. 139.

47

of ours, ever to share in the excitement and feel part of the great experiment of living in a new day the life of the Congregational Way? Indeed, how are the thousands of people who have always been Congregationalists, ever to have their interest stirred and their imaginations kindled to seek and learn and live this exciting way of church life?

One point surely, at which Congregationalism becomes concrete in the lives of its people, is precisely at the point where they join the church. This is the moment at which they "own" or give consent, to the covenant. This is the time, if it ever comes in their lives, when they reflect seriously on what it means to be a Christian, and what it means to be a Congregationalist. This is when they are most willing to try to live the new life, most willing to make the great promises of faith, most willing to learn of Christ's Church and to be a working, praying, living part of its life.

And yet, how many of our people say: "Why, when I joined the church I was simply told to be at service on such-and-such a Sunday, and I would be taken in. It was the easiest thing in the world!" Again and again this is the story: for some, even when they joined the Church for the first time; and for many, when they joined a second or third time by letter of transfer. No time of "fasting and prayer" as the Savoy Declaration requires; no searching of oneself; no concern about faith; no study of the Congregational Way; not even a meeting of the new members with each other for friendship's sake. In a Church Way that is committed to people, their life together in the congregation, and their peculiar relationship of direct responsibility to the Lord of the Church, what could be less Congregational?

The Congregational Way is the free way, the open way, the simple way, but it was never meant to be the *easy* way! If Congregationalism is to exist at all, it must be *difficult* to become a Congregationalist. Membership in one of our churches must never come cheaply. The time of joining must be a time of decision, a time of study, a season of prayer, an act of commitment.

One of the things we Americans too often forget is that even in England, or Scotland, or Australia becoming a Congregationalist is a sacrifice. Scotland's Church is the Presbyterian Church of Scotland, and England's Church the Episcopalian Church of England. They are the churches supported by the State. They are the ones who conduct official ceremonies. They are the ones whose outstanding preachers wear the scarlet cassock of the Chaplains to the Queen. And they are the ones whose church membership carries both church and community prestige.

Who then, would want to be a Congregationalist? Who would want to give up the community standing afforded him in the State Church in order to join the little free church down the way? The English Congregational churches receive no favors from the government. They are forced by law to support the State Church through their taxes whether they are members or not. "The Church" can mean only the State Church in England. Even their dead must be buried in Anglican church-yards. Congregationalists and other free churchmen are not officially allowed to take communion in the Church of England. Indeed, not until 1870 were Congregationalists even admitted to Oxford and Cambridge Universities.

To be a Congregationalist in Great Britain is to be part of a minority. It is to be the object of a very real discrimination. In situations like these it takes some conviction to join the Congregational Way. You have to care a great deal. You have to be deeply convinced of your stand. You have to really love the Lord and be ready to follow Him.

How many of us would be eager to be Congregationalists if any of this were true in America? In the Commonwealth of Massachusetts the Congregational churches are by far the largest and most influential of the Protestant denominations. In most communities they are "the" church. Among their members are the leading citizens. They have respect, prestige, prosperity. The fact is, it is rather comfortable being a Congregationalist in Massachusetts—or in almost any part of America.

But if there is no tension in becoming a member, no real valley of decision, no thoughtful consideration and study, what hope is there for the Congregational Way in America? How can there ever be a sense of adventure, a feeling that this is a peculiar and wonderful Way we have been called to follow, an awareness that this decision of becoming a Christian and a Congregationalist is of life-changing importance?

If men and women are to "own" a covenant, if they are to agree to walk together in love in the way of the Lord Jesus, then surely it is essential in our "Way" that at the time they join the Church they be given the opportunity to come into our fellowship as thoughtfully and as prayerfully as possible. The "fasting" that Savoy commends is perhaps a bit much for our day, but surely a crucial necessity is prayer.

The obligations and privileges of the Congregational Way can become concrete and alive then, at the point of joining the church. For it is here where those wanting to be members can be gathered together by the minister for several evenings, or perhaps for a number of weeks or months, to talk about Christian faith, about Congregationalism, and about the work and witness of the particular church they are joining. It is here that they can be helped to real insights into the Congregational Way, here that they can honestly face the responsibilities and privileges it puts upon them, here that they can give or renew their allegiance to Christ, and here that they can pray together and establish ties of Christian friendship with each other and with their pastor.

This is one of Congregationalism's greatest opportunities to raise up men and women who understand their destiny as a "covenant people." It is one point at which we quite concretely begin to live this special life of our Congregational Way.

And yet, if their only moment of insight and of conscious effort to live under the covenant were at the point of joining the Church, Congregationalists might well find their inspiration and sense of adventure fading as time passed. But the great fact is that the people of our Way have sincerely sought to live this covenant life in an institution known as the "Church Meeting."

This name may well have an unfamiliar ring for us Americans. "Church Meeting? What's that?" some will ask. "Another name for Church suppers and socials?" Far from that, the Church Meeting is "the" unique institution in Congregationalism.

It grew out of the conviction of the earliest Congregationalists that if Christ really meant that "Where two or three are gathered together in My Name, there am I in the midst of them," then it was in the gathered company of the two or three, meeting in love, that He could most directly, and powerfully, and personally govern His Church. The "Lordship of Christ" was no mere theological formula, nor any vague, idealistic, and impractical notion with them. Christ was the sovereign, the ruler of each local congregation. Their conviction was that if the people of a local church gathered together in a spirit of prayer, honestly seeking to know the Lord's will for them, He would come into their midst and guide their minds and hearts in such a way that they would all know what He intended them to do, and would furthermore be made of one mind in their determination to do it.

This was the sole reason for the defiance of that tiny band of Christians who met at Scrooby Manor near the end of the sixteenth century. They could stand up to Church and State only on this premise: that the One Who met with them and governed them at Scrooby was a higher authority and a truer sovereign than even the Queen and her church and bishops could be. "King of kings, and Lord of lords!"—that was their Jesus; and let no man stand in the way of that! No wonder they could never be stamped out. As long as they lived armored with that passionate conviction they were invincible.

They didn't need bishops and canon laws. Christ was enough. He was their practical discipline and direct authority, as well as their Saviour and their Lord. Indeed, it was only this relationship that gave any excuse for Congregationalism at all. To have thrown over all the checks and balances, the disciplines and authority of episcopacy would have been mad. Congregationalism would indeed have been an anarchy. But they set aside the laws and authority of men only so they could submit themselves obediently to a higher law and a higher authority: the law and authority of Jesus Christ.

The Congregational Church Meeting then is the whole people of God in a given local church meeting together and governing themselves under the guidance of Christ. It sounds completely naive and idealistic. "How can you be so arrogant," the skeptics say, "as to think that Christ would be there at your little meeting actually telling you what to say and how to vote, so that you can announce to the world that you have done His will? Ridiculous! It could never work."

Arrogant or not, this is what Jesus promised to do and this is what our forefathers testified again and again that He *had* done when they said so many times: "It seemed good to us and to the Holy Spirit . . ."

I do not mean it is always with a rush of mighty wind from heaven and with tongues of fire as it was at Pentecost —though I quite believe it could be. I mean only that when Christian people meet together actually expecting the Lord to be there; actually expecting Him to hear, and to judge, and to lead them; they find when all is done that indeed, they were not alone; that a strange and wonderful Spirit had seemed to be among them; and that their decisions ring in their hearts with a peculiarly unshakable and unanimous conviction.

The Church Meeting that none of us will ever forget here in Williamsburg concerned the building of a Sunday School addition to our church. The Parish had been meeting in small groups to study the plans and to pray about them. It was a concern that had been part of our prayers in our worship services and in our private prayers as individuals for weeks. We had no classrooms for our Sunday

School and many felt we desperately needed them. But the feeling was by no means unanimous. Finally the whole congregation met to make the decision. The cost presented by the Building Committee was fierce. The vestry was crowded. All shades of opinion were represented. It could have been a hassle. But the meeting began in prayer. They asked the Lord to be there. They heard all sides. And before they left, this little congregation had voted to raise the money and build the building. Person after person confessed to me later that they had come ready to blast the whole idea, but that during the meeting they had become strangely convinced that God wanted us to build. The decision was unanimous, and there is not one of us in the church today who does not believe that Christ was there, that our decision was His will, and that He has been with us every step of the way since.

The Lord moves in strange and wondrous ways—and He has promised to do it every time we meet expecting Him! It is the way a church meets that counts. No ordinary business meeting will do. It must be a meeting for worship. Indeed, it must begin with actual worship led by the minister—at least Scripture reading and prayer. Probably a Church Meeting can have Roberts' Rules, motions, amendments, and all the rest. But the important thing is the attitude of the people: the attitude of expectancy; the attitude of openness—of having eyes to see and ears to hear; and the attitude of accepting one another—of loving each one of these people as another child of God, of believing that the Spirit can speak that night through any one of them, and of being sincerely ready to hear what they have to say. It is also the attitude of coming to the meeting to do Christ's will and not your own.

This last is the hardest. No man dare come to a Church Meeting convinced that he already has the answer to questions that will be raised, and with an iron-bound determination to vote through his idea come what may. Only if the people believe that the Lord has a will for them which might be different from their own wills, can the Congregational Church Meeting succeed. It is the last place in the world for "railroading." The will of Christ *could* be spoken through a minority of only one person. The will of Christ is not to be simply identified with the opinion of the majority. It is a will above their own which through prayer and the spirit of love can make itself known through the people. In the Congregational Church Meeting no close votes or even two-thirds majorities will do.

This is why the tradition of the Church Meeting is that every decision must be unanimous. For after all, what good is a great decision unless the whole people of God proclaim it together, and believe in it, and support it with all their hearts?

So many churches—in all denominations—are so often involved in "fights"; fights over this or that, in which some are offended and perhaps leave the church, or worse still, simply withdraw from its life and brood for years in anger. Almost always they are over *little* things—shamefully little things. Someone wants to do it this way, another that. Or perhaps, as occasionally happens in rural churches, a family feud breaks out in the church. The instances could be multiplied a thousand-fold. The point is that such fights— or even minor tensions—have tempted churches into thinking that divided votes and narrow majorities are perfectly acceptable, even useful, in the Christian Church.

This is perhaps especially tempting to Congregationalists,

where important church decisions must be acted upon by the members themselves. "Why, we could never get everyone to agree," they often cry, "and after all, some disagreement is good democracy, isn't it?" The idea of church people being unanimous in all their decisions just seems impossible and impractical to us.

And yet, in the tradition of the Church Meeting as practiced by our cousins in British Congregationalism, this is not only possible, but it is the accepted norm. "A Church Meeting should be *different* from other meetings!" is their cry. "A town meeting, or a business meeting can get along on majority decisions, but not a Church Meeting."

If a given decision is Christ's will, then it is His will for all the people. It is not something that can be divided. Therefore, Congregationalists who live in this tradition are willing to have their church meet again and again and again—over the same issue—until all the people are convinced and ready to stand together in the knowledge that they have been led indeed, by the Holy Spirit.

But this kind of spirit among the people of a church is possible only if they see their "Meeting" as more than a business meeting. They must regard it as worship. Indeed, as the acting out of the demands put upon them by God through the preaching of the Word in morning worship. This is why in England the "Meeting" sometimes comes after a Sunday worship service of preaching and the Lord's Supper, followed by a common parish meal. The meeting then occupies the afternoon as a kind of extension of the morning's worship. In many places this is not practically possible, but it can always be conducted within the framework of worship. And if the people come understanding that the work of the Church Meeting is to be done prayer-

fully, in love for one another and for God, then their ulti-
mate decisions *can* be unanimous.

This does *not* mean that the Meeting is without discussion and differences of opinion; that all are to think and
feel exactly the same about specific issues. It *does* mean
that "the Meeting" cares for the feelings and convictions
of each person there, and will never be satisfied to pass
anything until even the least of these is glad and of one
mind with them.

The other thing that can make this spirit come is the
meeting *often* of the gathered church—not just an annual
meeting once a year! Christian people, members of the
same church, must meet together often enough to know
each other; often enough to know each other's deep concerns, differences in view-point, and special needs. You
cannot love a man you do not know. You cannot achieve
unanimity of spirit with someone with whom you have not
talked and prayed. The Congregational Church Meeting
then must be for worship as well as business, and must
meet often.

The trouble is, that for us Americans, the whole idea
sounds like too much work. "It would take all night to get
anything done under that system!" we say . . . "It would
take too long. We have too much to do to sit around talking for half the night!" And of course, anything more frequent than our annual "corporation" meeting seems a terrible imposition. "Too busy," "too slow," "too inefficient"
are our protests.

And yet, it is busyness and desire for efficiency that so
often kill the great movements of the Spirit. It is so easy to
be too busy to know your neighbor, too busy to love people,
and too busy to wait quietly before God.

The quiet knowledge, the love, and the openness toward God are the characteristics of Congregationalism at its best. It is these which are the great traditions in our heritage, and these which have in the past and can still in the future make the Congregational Way the way of the Covenant People.

3. Freedom Bound by Love

Probably there is nothing that we Americans prize more than freedom. Freedom is our heritage. In many ways it is the meaning of America.

But freedom is more than America's heritage. It is the Congregational heritage as well. Indeed, Congregationalism has had a great deal to do with the bringing of freedom to America. We do not always appreciate that when John Carver, standing on the deck of the *Mayflower*, was elected governor of Plymouth Colony it was more than just the democratic institution of the New England Town Meeting that was being born. The significant fact is that this English Congregationalist, chosen largely by his Congregational brethren, was the first colonial governor in the New World, and perhaps the first in history, ever to be chosen by the people themselves in a free election.[1]

Congregationalists have always rejoiced in this heritage which they brought to America, and have been grateful to represent—perhaps more than any other way of church life —the way of freedom. Probably no other institution in

[1] Partially quoted from George F. Willson, *The Pilgrim Reader*, p. 101.

America has stood so consistently for the principle of freedom of life as have the Congregational churches.

Oh, we have our black marks all right. We remember to our shame how once we condoned in Salem the hanging of witches, how in self-righteous arrogance we drove through the streets of Boston Quaker women stripped to the waist and publicly shamed for their faith. We remember the hair-splitting of the Half-Way Covenant, and the sometimes narrow spirit which played its part in the Unitarian departure. Our need of forgiveness is real indeed.

But from the prison days of early Congregationalism in Britain, and from the ringing appeal at Savoy for tolerance of all Christian brothers, and from the courageous pilgrimage of the Plymouth adventure, down through the town-meeting tradition of New England villages, the impassioned concern for universal education, the founding of the missionary enterprise, and on to our modern concern for the freedom of churches and of people in faith and polity, the Way of Congregationalism has been the way of a steady and often daring defense of the principle of freedom.

And yet the sorrow of modern Congregationalism in America is that we have lost our understanding of the real meaning of Congregational freedom. We haven't forgotten about freedom. Indeed, we have made it our watch-word and flown its banner high whenever we could. Many among us have even taken the defense of freedom to be their marching orders and have done courageous battle in its cause.

But we have believed Congregationalism and its freedom to be a kind of rank individualism. We have told ourselves that the freedom of the Congregational Way was freedom *from:* freedom *from* bishops, freedom *from* the coils of denominational red tape, freedom *from* creeds, *from* pressure, *from* programs—freedom from everything!

More than once I have been told: "The thing I like about Congregationalism is that a person can believe anything he wants!" Or, "The good thing about this denomination is that no one can tell us what to do." Indeed, there is a widespread feeling that even within a given congregation there is no need for the individual to hold any great conviction of faith or practice in common with the other members of the church. In the minds of thousands of Congregationalists is the idea that a Congregational church can be a gathered conglomeration of free-thinking individuals bound together only by their conviction that they should be free.

But Congregationalism is *not* simply freedom *from.* It is neither a simple freedom from ecclesiastical controls, nor even the right to order our life as congregations any way we happen to choose. The freedom of the Congregational Way is freedom *from* the rule of men only so that we can be more completely obedient to the rule of Christ. The Congregational fathers at Savoy were not interested in living without authority. It wasn't authority from which the Scrooby congregation had been fleeing when they sailed for Holland and later for America. Their objection was to the wrong kind of authority—the authority of men.

They knew human nature and the subtlety of sin too well to harbor any illusions about the pure motives and incorruptibility of men—even good men—in high places. They knew very well that power corrupts. And they understood better than most the peculiar temptations of ecclesiastical power. They sensed the all too easy rationalizations open to those who believe their cause to be God's cause, and their will, God's will. They had no doubt that the men of the established church who had persecuted, and hunted, and imprisoned them had done it completely in the conviction that God was on their side and that Separatists were heretics who must be wiped out. Indeed, they remembered that no less a man than Saul of Tarsus had once tracked down Christians and taken their lives in the name of God!

Let others place authority in the hands of popes and priests if they would, but Congregationalists would trust a higher authority. This is why they sought to be free! Not to do as they wished, not to believe anything at all, not to live without principles, and discipline, and integrity. They hungered for a better discipline, a purer principle, an incorruptible authority. They wanted Christ—Christ alone: Christ the Lord of the Church; Christ the King of the realm; Christ Who alone could rule directly, righteously, lovingly, eternally. The Church polity they envisioned was no anarchy. It was not strictly democracy. It could easily be called authoritarianism: the absolute authority of Jesus Christ; the absolute authority of the One Who said: "I am the Good Shepherd Who lays down his life for the sheep"; "I am the door, (and) if any man enter in he shall be saved"; "I am the Way, the Truth, and the Life"; and "I am the Alpha and the Omega, the beginning and the end." This was the kind of authority they wanted. The authority that no man can exercise. The authority that Christ alone does exercise, in power and in love.

This is how the earliest Congregationalists conceived of their freedom. It was freedom to obey the only One who deserved to be obeyed; freedom to be open as congregations to the invasion of his Holy Spirit; freedom to know and feel the power of that Spirit; and freedom to be guided, and governed, and humbled, and taught by that Spirit.

They wanted to live their life as congregations: as local, gathered churches free of all ecclesiastical authority and therefore free to accept the full burden of their Christian responsibility upon themselves. It was here, they believed, in the local congregation, that the church was truly the Church. It was here, if ever, that men and women would be converted to Christ. It was here, if ever, that they would learn to love Him and one another. It was here, if ever, that the real power of the Church would be. And it was here that the real imagination and insight of the Church would flourish, that the greatest missionary work would be done, that the deepest fellowship would be known, where Christ could most powerfully touch the lives of men, and where the Kingdom itself would come.

If the Church was to be great anywhere, it must be great in the gathered congregation of Christ's people. If it does not have the Spirit there, it will not have it anywhere else. And for all the papal encyclicals, all the decrees of bishops, all the programs and goals of denominational officials, the church of Christ without the Spirit will be no more than the grass of the field which today is and tomorrow will be cast into the oven—dried up, useless, and fit only to be burned.

All this the fathers of Congregationalism knew, and we must know it too. "The liberty wherewith Christ hath made us free" they knew to be for a great purpose—a purpose which could only be fulfilled where men gather face to face with each other and with their Lord. Freedom, they believed, was something that must be lived out where life is most personal and most responsible. For there, among the two or three gathered around Christ in love, is the highest obedience and therefore the truest and the widest freedom.

Congregational freedom was meant to be the freedom of the covenant: the freedom of a voluntary agreement with Christ and with our fellow Christians to walk together in love—to obey the Lord and to care for the brethren with concern not for the word of man, but only for the Word of the Lord.

In other words, our freedom is "freedom bound by love." It is a freedom which is open and wide, and yet disciplined by our love for Christ and our love for our fellow-Christians through Christ. For Jesus said, "A new commandment I give unto you, that ye love one another, as I have loved you. . . ."

It is this kind of freedom that Christ gave not just to Congregationalists in the seventeenth century, but to the whole Church at the very beginning of its life. For the way of freedom was the New Testament way. It was the way those early churches of Ephesus, and Corinth, and Thessalonica, and Rome lived with each other. For their power came from within. It came from the Lord Himself in-dwelling their lives and their congregations and giving them power not only to live the Christian life themselves, but to proclaim it throughout the lands of the empire.

The New Testament Church was a great Church; great because it was free; great because its freedom was the freedom of faithful obedience.

This was the life to which our forefathers were called. This is the life to which we are called. Let no man take lightly, nor scorn to defend what has been so generously given. Freedom is our inheritance. It is the Way in which

God has called us, as Congregationalists, to walk. Especially it is the way of this better freedom—the freedom bound by love.

But how does this freedom manifest itself in the Congregational Way of church life? In what particular ways are we free?

Most obvious is our freedom of government. Government in Congregationalism is direct and authoritative from Christ the Lord of the Church, to each one of His local gathered churches. It is not from Christ through an authoritative hierarchy to people as the Roman Catholics conceive it, nor from Christ through an apostolic succession of bishops to congregations as the Anglicans see it, nor even democratically from Christ through presbyteries to churches as the Presbyterians might define it.

Because of this direct line of authority to churches from their Lord, our Way is known as "Independency," and our churches as "free" churches. We are "independent" of other churches and of the councils of the denomination, and we are "free" of both ecclesiastical and civil control.

In English Congregationalism, where these terms are more often used, they are even more relevant than they are in America. For in Britain the churches of the Congregational Way are not only free from ecclesiastical controls within their fellowship, as we are, but they are also independent of and without any support from the national government and its official Church. Independency in Britain means a certain courage to venture forth from the safe confines of State protection and social acceptability into a life in which Christians and their churches are cast completely upon each other and upon their Lord. This life they live in contrast to the State Church of England which enjoys the protection, royal recognition, and financial help of a queen and her parliament.

There is no question with us of accepting State support, so freedom in America means, not freedom from political control, but freedom from ecclesiastical control. And yet, though our situations are slightly different, the courageous example of English Congregationalism continues to be an inspiration to freedom-loving Christians of the Congregational Way in America.

Our Congregational freedom of government means essentially that each Congregational Church is free before God to order its own life as it may feel directed by the Holy Spirit. No tradition is sacrosanct, save our freedom itself and our moral and spiritual obligation to be honestly open to the movement of the Spirit. No one way of doing things can ever be handed to us as a decree or order. Our way is to accept any suggestions and help offered as long as the Spirit leads us to think it is a wise thing to do and something God wants for the particular church we serve. If, on the other hand, the programs of the denomination seem not to be best for an individual church, that church feels under no obligation to accept it. It is the Spirit Himself Who will show us the way.

There is a sense in which we are under *no* obligation to the Church at large. We are meant to be free within each local, gathered church. Yet, in another sense, our obligation is very great. What if the Spirit is speaking to us through some word from the wider fellowship? What if He is using it in some instance to teach and lead our individual church? We are under obligation to be very careful that no word from the fellowship is carelessly rejected. Any word deserves our thoughtful, prayerful consideration.

Then if we vote no, we do it under God and with a clear conscience.

The tragedy in Congregationalism today, however, is that so many churches do not dare to live in this precarious and courageous freedom. They seem afraid to submit themselves to Christ's special will for them, and to launch out as pioneers into creative Christian adventures in the parishes where they were set to witness.

Denominational executives and councils can help. By the power of this same Spirit in their deliberations they can stir up new thinking. They can raise our sights. But their work is "in general." They plan for great masses of churches all across the land. They cannot know what God wants desperately to do in some given community. They cannot tell what miracles He might perform in some little church here, or in a great church there. They do not even know the great things already being done in a particular church. Yearbook statistics tell almost nothing!—almost nothing of the lives changed, the people helped, the Word preached, and the visions seen.

The only ones who can really know are the people themselves—the gathered people of God in each individual church. This is the meaning of our freedom! We are free because it is here where men and women live and worship and work face to face that the Spirit of Christ can work the most amazing wonders in the life of the Church. It is here, in the *churches*, that the great deeds can be done, the significant experiments tried. This is the place where one man can catch a vision, inspire others, and lead a people to do such things as they had never dared to do before. Here is where barriers of misunderstanding and hatred are broken down, and where all the social and personal tensions of our society converge and can be transformed by the creative power of a Spirit-filled community. No amount of denominational suggestion or promotion can even begin to do what churches like these can do.

It is our privilege, our responsibility, our eternal challenge, then, as churches of the Congregational Way, to order our own life. This means that everything—our committees, our men's work, our women's work, our buildings, our Bible-study, our prayer-life, everything—is ours to order, ours to conceive, ours to fashion according to the leading of Christ's Spirit.

One church may be quite different from another, because God's Will for each may be quite different. But in each case it will be His will defining and limiting any selfish use of that freedom. This is the glory of our Way! This is the wonderful challenge and opportunity that faces each one of our churches. A challenge that may mean great variety in our life, but one which also means power.

It is this variety itself which is a source of strength in the Congregational Way: for among us there are possible many different witnesses to meet different situations.

The great fact in the working of the Spirit in our churches is that a Congregational church lives or dies by the dedication and devotion of its people. Whenever it ceases to have people who care, it will cease to carry on and be a church. As in no other Way of church life, the church is the people, and freedom places a terrible and wonderful responsibility upon them.

That responsibility is probably felt most keenly in *the mission* of a Congregational church. For this is more than an area of responsibility. It is an area of imagination and inspiration of the people themselves.

What can a church be and do here without inspired laymen? It is one thing to say that the great work of the Church is done in local churches. It is one thing to say that we want to be free from the pall of denominational bureaucracy. But who is going to *do* the Lord's work in the local church? We cherish our freedom, but unless there are sincere and committed people with a vision of a great work to be done, nothing *will* be done.

It is so terribly easy for Congregational people to use freedom as license for having no mission at all. We were the denomination that founded the foreign missionary enterprise in America, and yet are we known today among Protestants as the people of zeal? Are we the ones who are always thought of as evangelical in our passion to win men to Christ? Are we the denomination whose churches give half their goods to the support of missions? Hardly!

We have far to go, and the leadership we need is of ordinary people who care; people who know that churches with no mission soon are dead; people who dare to stand up in Church Meeting and plead for an honored place for missions in the budget; and people who are willing to serve on missionary committees and to give themselves to educating and persuading their fellow Christians to the great needs not only of Africa and Turkey, but also of America— its slums, its schools, its migrant workers, and its poor.

Wherever a church is doing something really significant in its ministry to the community around it or in its concern for the Christian mission in other countries, it is always some inspired layman at the heart of it with the imperative of the Spirit about him, who is challenging, urging, laboring and making it a living reality. We demand freedom to govern ourselves, but that freedom is meaningless unless, as a people committed to Christ, we *fill* it with meaning.

And yet it is a serious thing to claim freedom as we claim it. Indeed, it sounds nearly presumptuous to say that God will lead us. "How do you know it is God Who leads you?" our critics say. "Chances are it is just some strong-willed person imposing his will on the rest of the meeting. How can you be sure? How can you order your whole church life on such a concept? That's no government, that's anarchy!"

But our fathers had an answer for this, and it is their answer which must be our answer. "The Bible will keep us true," they said. "The Bible is the check upon our freedom. The Spirit speaking through the Word will keep us from going off on tangents. It will bring us back to the heart of our faith and to the core of our mission."

And that is true. The Bible itself is our book of rules, the law of our life. Why should we devise canon laws when we have the Bible?

If a Congregational church gathers together frequently in Church Meeting; if it begins that meeting prayerfully before the open Bible, aware of its power to judge as well as to heal; if it is sincerely willing to follow Christ's will and not its own, and believes that that will can be made known in the Meeting; and if it believes that Christ's nature, His way of thinking, the demands He makes upon men, and His dearest hopes for their lives are revealed for all to see in the pages of the New Testament: then the Bible can be in fact, a powerful instrument of discipline and faith in the life of that church. The Bible, regarded and revered in this way, can be the check and balance upon all a free church does.

Here in the Bible is the discipline and love by which we of the Congregational Way can honestly say that ours is the Way not only of freedom, but of freedom bound by love.

There is another way too that love binds our freedom to keep us from narrow provincialism and from the wrong kind of self-sufficiency. It is a way into which our freedom itself leads us. For when we are free to be ourselves, free to go apart and fashion our lives as churches in the most creative way we can, we are also free as churches to form any kind of Christian fellowship into which we may feel led by the Spirit.

And this is what Congregationalism has done both in England and America. Savoy itself was the gathering-together of men of like mind who sensed that, in their individual churches, they shared a common "Way" of life, and felt a need to come together to agree on the great truths of their Way and to give mutual support and strength to one another. Mutual encouragement was much needed in those days of conflict. It was also needed for sheer reasons of Christian friendship. And so today English Congregationalists meet together in the fellowship both of county unions and of the Congregational Union of England and Wales.

In America, too, the churches of the Congregational Way soon felt the need to meet together for reasons of friendship and common concern. John Robinson had counseled his Separatist congregation before ever they left England to join with the Puritans when they reached the New World. It was little wonder then, especially amid the lonely life of the Massachusetts wilderness in the years following 1620, that the Separatists of Plymouth Colony and the Puritans of Massachusetts Bay should gravitate toward each other in friendship, and soon form a new stream of Congregationalism on the American continent.

From this early beginning in Massachusetts Congregationalism spread west to the Berkshires and south along the Connecticut River under the leadership of Thomas Hooker to Hartford. It reached also the Connecticut coast at New Haven, and became the dominant church throughout New England. Through the nineteenth century especially, the Congregational Way moved west until today the mid-west and the west-coast regions of America share with New England the distinction of being important centers of Congregational life.

Very early in its life on American soil Congregationalism felt the need for ties of fellowship and understanding between local churches. The Cambridge synod in 1648 was probably the first such gathering, and in it ministers and churches met to define and proclaim the great convictions of faith and order which they believed and practiced in common.

Another kind of gathering for fellowship as well as for business began to grow up quite naturally among the churches. These were the ecclesiastical councils called for the examination and ordination or installation of a minister. New England's churches, as an act of fellowship, and as a way of keeping high the standards of their ministry, made a practice of inviting the pastors and delegates of neighboring churches to come on an appointed day to examine on matters of faith and experience the pastor the given church had called, and to proceed with that church in his ordination or installation. Always the request came from the local church and was sent out by letter as an invitation to the other churches. They were invited in as friends to share in this special occasion in the life of one of their sister churches. They came with no superior authority, nor did they try to wield such.

It was from these occasional councils that our modern associations grew. To this day Congregationalism all across the country is divided into natural geographical areas, within which the churches of this common way feel a close kinship and a common interest. Not that a central body ever set up arbitrarily the lines of these divisions. They grew naturally, and were often divided by a river here, a row of hills there, or perhaps a valley in between. It was out of freedom that they grew—a freedom of local churches to bind themselves in friendship with whom they would. And certainly, it was out of a freedom which knew well that independency needed fellowship, and that physical and spiritual isolation could mean death for such an ever-growing and open institution as a Christian church.

So associations have become the vital heart of the life of fellowship among people of our Way in America. This is where the most meaningful forms of Christian friendship and cooperative effort beyond the local church have taken place. Because it is in the associations that the lay people of different churches know each other best. And it is here that the ministers too, often of varying theological position and interest, know each other as Christian friends and understand and love each other as they might never otherwise.

Hampshire Association, centering in the Pioneer Valley of Massachusetts and stretching over the Pelham hills to the east and into the Berkshire hills to the west, has meant more to my little church and to me than can possibly be said. "Our churches are so close they touch," one minister told me when first I came to Williamsburg. And it is true. They touched not only geographically, but their hearts touched too. There is a love and understanding among these churches and people that is rare and precious to us all. In a period of heated feelings and strong convictions about the future of Congregationalism throughout the denomination, men of opposite views have been upheld by their basic respect and regard for each other, and have been able to discuss differences rationally and helpfully. When delegates are to be chosen for national meetings, a sincere effort is always made to choose men and women representing all positions on the great issues expected to arise.

In this atmosphere of honest appreciation and regard it has been possible to maintain high standards of the ministry. The churches and their ministers really come to ordinations and installations. They ask questions of candidates seeking ministerial standing, not to trap, but to help. And of all the young ministers who have come to serve churches here, not one has been allowed to embark upon his ministry among us without the feeling that he was being supported, and strengthened, and shepherded by his ministerial brethren in the Association and by their people.

Such a fellowship becomes alive and creative in a hundred ways and gives an added depth to our freedom—the depth of a freedom which here again is bound by love.

But over the years there was felt the need for still another expression of fellowship beyond the life of the local church in the state and national conferences.

As Congregationalism spread over more and more of the country, the urge grew for ministers and people of state and regional areas to meet together. There were ideas to be exchanged, encouragement to be given, work to be done

—all of which made quite natural the growth not only of state conferences but also the National Council, known now as the General Council.

In each case these have been free associations formed to serve the churches, with the idea always that they were servants of the local churches and in no sense their masters. Ours is not an ascending hierarchy. A state conference is formed by all the churches of a state to *help* them: to give guidance in Christian education and to give them a means for carrying on together certain projects they cannot do as easily alone.

Delegates sent to a state conference are assumed at those meetings to *be* the conference, to vote as a conference, and to bear sole responsibility for the decisions of that meeting. Anything voted at such a meeting can have no binding effect on local churches. It can come only as a recommendation either to be rejected by the churches or to be accepted and entered into cooperatively.

Our General Council, a national gathering meeting every two years, has essentially the same relation to the churches. It neither speaks for them nor can bind them by its actions. Delegates sent from local churches are members of the Council on their *own*. The *churches* they represent are *not* members of the Council. And again the actions taken have only the authority of recommendations as far as binding local churches or conferences or associations. This is what is meant when Congregationalists say that they are part of a "fellowship." Our actions taken together are done willingly and in love—not by coercion nor by any form of higher authority.

The legislative way of Congregationalism is the Way of the Spirit. It is by the persuasion of the Spirit in the Meeting that a local church becomes convinced that God is calling them to some particular task or to some special decision. It is a question among us whether the Spirit can move in the same way at all in the larger occasional councils: for there the delegates are committed to each other in no sense as are the members of a local church who are bound to each other geographically, emotionally, and spiritually in a permanent fellowship.

But assuming that He does sometimes speak to the heart of a great council, it is only as He speaks that same word to the heart of the local gathered church that the decision of the great council has authority for that church.

It is this point at which every Congregational church is under obligation to "test the Spirit," and to be open to His persuasion. And woe to our churches in America if they know not the signs of this Spirit in their life! Woe to them if they do not cultivate this attitude of openness and seeking which only the Church Meeting gives! And woe to us all if we forget the Spirit altogether, for then our Way becomes meaningless, our authority is gone, and our freedom is lost! Only the Spirit of Christ and the sincere intention of His people to obey His will can keep the fellowship of the Congregational Way a real fellowship. Only Christ with us, and our willingness to follow him can make this system work. We need the services of the conference and of the General Council's Social Action, Missionary, Service Committees, Pension Boards and other helps. But we use them best, and support them most generously, when the tie that binds is the tie of love, wrought by the Spirit.

There are few other forms of denominational life like this where freedom makes possible so many creative forms of fellowship and binds them close by love and not by law.

This means too, that any number of less formal relations are possible. Associations of ministers, gatherings for common concern, local missionary enterprises—a thousand possibilities for fellowship and service are open to those of the Congregational Way by the freedom in which the Holy Spirit leads.

Beyond the local and national levels of Associations and the General Council there is the "ecumenical" movement of cooperation and merger across both denominational and national lines in which Congregationalists are interested and involved. Congregationalism, in its freedom, has been open to recognizing the gifts of other denominations and to cooperating and sometimes merging with them in the work of serving Christ's Kingdom.

Our freedom has made possible wide experimentation in interdenominational cooperation, especially at the local level. Some of these ventures—in a place like the East Harlem Protestant Parish in New York City, in cooperative ministries to college students, in theological education, in rural larger parishes and federated churches—have been some of the most imaginative and creative in our time. These experiments have demonstrated the finest and certainly the most effective kind of ecumenicity.

Their genius has been Congregationalism's freedom to adapt itself, sometimes radically, to local situations and particular needs. Our very ability to proceed "on the spot" without "going through headquarters" has been a great strength to our witness rather than a weakness.

While Congregationalism has been utterly committed to

this ideal of being "of one Spirit" with all Christians on this first level, its leaders have been active in the ecumenical movement on the international level, primarily through the work of the World Council of Churches. They feel very deeply the call to promote actual mergers of churches until the divisions within Protestantism are healed and perhaps even some day our separation from Rome itself.

Although many in our Way do not share their optimism nor their driving concern to effect these "united churches" immediately, nevertheless the concern is widespread among nearly all Congregationalists that "they may be one even as Thou and I are one . . ." Already ministers and people of the Congregational Way feel a oneness with all Christians and cooperate with them, and accept them, wherever those other Christians permit it. Already we accept the ordination of ministers of other denominations as valid before God. We do not re-ordain the many men who come into our "Way" from other fellowships. Already we welcome "all who love the Lord Jesus" to His Table in our Communion services.

Our very "Way" itself is founded upon the ecumenical principle—if the above-quoted words from Jesus' prayer are accepted to *be* that principle. Our original separation from the Church of England was in protest against that church's un-ecumenical spirit and practice.

The principles which are basic to the life of the Christian Church, especially as seen in its New Testament life, are the very heart and life of the Congregational Way. The early Church was guided by the Holy Spirit, and we take this guidance as our one authority and discipline. Our "Church Meeting" was conceived precisely as an instrument which would lend itself to the honest movement of the Spirit in our midst when as churches we are gathered together as two or three in the name of the Lord. The only reason for our freedom is so that we can be open to this leading of the Spirit. Our theological convictions on ordination and communion—the two greatest problems in the ecumenical movement today—are based on the conviction that it is the Spirit, not we, who ordains and who invites to the table. We believe Christ does His work by making His will known through the whole congregation— thus our name "Congregationalists," and thus our actual living in our every-day life as churches the principle of the priesthood of *all* believers.

Many of us feel that far from being obligated, as some leaders say, "to go out of existence" to promote the ecumenical cause, the Congregational Way, by its very ecumenical nature as free, and open, and dependent upon the Spirit, has within itself a very great gift to offer this movement of World Christianity—that with our covenant life, our "freedom bound by love" we preserve in principle the very basis on which the ecumenical movement can unite.

This principle of fellowship is one more of the creative directions in which Congregationalism, in its freedom, has been able to go.

One of the most thrilling privileges of our freedom is the important one of being able to offer Christian service under the guidance of the spirit. This has been perhaps the most creative result of the impact of the Congregational Way upon American life. Never have we had prescribed denominational patterns to follow, never any iron-clad rules of procedure, and never any central offices through which every project conceived by a Congregationalist had to be cleared. The people of this Way have been free to respond to any human need that touched their hearts, or any cause that roused their concern. Where the Spirit has led we have been free to follow.

Over a hundred and fifty years ago, in the year 1806, five young men were walking across a field near the campus of Williams College. Suddenly, thunder crashed about them and a torrent of rain began to fall. The boys took shelter under the nearest haystack. Exactly what happened there we cannot be sure. But we do know that under that haystack in the driving rain of that day a prayer-meeting took place which was to send those boys to the ends of the earth as America's first foreign missionaries.

They were only college students, but they gave America both her first Board of Foreign Missions and her first Bible Society! The Holy Spirit could lead those young Congregationalists because they were free to follow.

From the days of the Massachusetts Bay Colony until now, this has been the adventuring spirit of the Congregational Way that has pioneered in new forms of Christian service. Where other ways were often bound by ecclesiastical law and procedures, the Congregational Way has been an open channel in which God could act directly and with great power.

But missions were not the only area in which the Spirit led our fathers into fields of service. Their concern was also with education. In a day when Christianity is so eagerly kept out of education it might be well to remember the words of our Congregational forebears which stand inscribed over the gates of Harvard College to this day:

"After God had carried us safe to New England and we had builded our houses . . . reared convenient places for God's worship, and settled the civil government: One of the next things we longed for and looked after was to advance learning and perpetuate it to Posterity. . . ." *

That was the spirit that not only gave us Harvard College, but also Yale, Dartmouth, Amherst, Oberlin, and a host of other colleges across the country. Nor did these Congregational pioneers in education want a narrow sectarianism. One by one, nearly all of these colleges have thrown open their doors to students of every religion and background. It was the vision of a wider contribution to the work of the whole kingdom that brought an end to denominationalism in these and others of our colleges. And this act in itself was possible because of Congregationalism's freedom.

Pioneering projects in Christian service in many parts of America—from Negro education at Tougaloo and Tuskegee to the work of the East Harlem Protestant Parish in New York, bear the marks of the Holy Spirit at work in the freedom of the Congregational Way!

It is the same moving power that in the little church I know best has stirred a missionary zeal that has begun to care about near-by migrants and far-off refugees and orphans, has taught something of the joy of Christian giving, has made homes and church themselves a mission in receiving Negro children from the city for summer vacations, and has

* Partially quoted from George F. Wilson, *The Pilgrim Reader*, p. 101.

sent both men and women into the wards of a mental hospital to serve.

It is a Spirit able to make our Congregational fellowship a continuing and moving power in the life of this land. I pray it will never cease to blow as a clear fresh wind from heaven in the life of every one of our churches, and that it may raise up among us a new generation of Christians who will be mighty in the service of the Kingdom.

For the freedom of the Congregational Way is not dead. It will live and grow in power as long as we remember that it is not a freedom from authority, but a freedom to be utterly obedient to the greatest authority of all. A freedom completely free, because it is completely bound by love for Christ. It is this kind of freedom under the Spirit which is our great gift to Christ's whole Church today. It is this kind of freedom which God means us to defend with our lives.

4. "Jesus Is Lord!"

Freedom is a great heritage. Whether as a citizen in a democracy, or as a churchman amid all the complexities of organization and polity, freedom is a priceless privilege. But in matters of faith, freedom can be a problem.

The Roman Catholic has no question about what he believes. The dogma of his church is drummed home to him from an early age and he can say "Here is where I stand." The Episcopalian can say "I believe in God the Father Almighty, Maker of heaven and earth, and in Jesus Christ His only Son. . . ." without a question. It is right there in the creed. Even the Presbyterian, freer than most, can hand out the Westminster Confession and say "Here it is—the essence of our faith!"

But what about the Congregationalist—the free churchman? What can he say when pressed to tell what his people believe? Sometimes, it is a little embarrassing to be a Congregationalist.

You can answer, "Well . . . now *I* believe . . ." But that begs the question. "We know what you believe," your friends will say, "but what do all the *other* Congregationalists believe? What does your *denomination* stand for, in matters of faith?"

This is an embarrassing question because, quite honestly, the answer is elusive. Who can speak for the *other* followers of a way of church life which *has* no single creed or confession of faith for the denomination as a whole? What can anyone say of a "way" which includes in one fellowship such tremendous freedom and diversity in all things?

Look at us. Some of our pastors mount their pulpits every Sunday in all the regalia of clerical collar, geneva bands, and academic hood, while others refuse to wear anything more than a plain business suit or simple robe! One of our churches has a symbolic and ritual liturgy the equal of many an Episcopal or Lutheran church, while another features the plain evangelical preaching service of one of the most prominent fundamentalist churches in the country. Half our churches have the high center pulpit, plain communion table, and bare meeting-house of the old puritanism, while the other half have often the divided chancel and high altar of the more recent liturgical interest.

But this variety made possible by our freedom is not just a matter of polity or practice. It is also true of our faith. Here a congregation may repeat the Apostles' Creed every Sunday while there another church may scarcely speak the name of God. Easter Sunday among us may find one preacher proclaiming the Resurrection of Christ, and another settling for the true but hardly comparable new life of spring—the story not of Christ the Lord, but of flowers, and birds, and trees.

Now, thank God for our freedom to *be* different. Thank God for our freedom to think for ourselves, to follow the leading of Christ's Spirit, to be open to new revelations, and not bound rigidly to archaic laws and formulations of the past!

84

But what do we hold in common? What high ground of faith can we stand on together and cry to the world: "Here is the faith that unites us as a Christian fellowship. This we believe, and—so help us God—we can believe no other!"

This is *the* crucial question in Congregationalism today. The question of whether or not, in the midst of our treasured freedom and tolerance, there actually is a deep, and consuming, and passionate faith that binds us all together in spirit, and gives us power as a fellowship of churches.

There are many who have doubts about this. They worship in three or four of our churches and they begin to wonder. They attend two Easter services and come away asking: "But can there be two Gospels? *Is* there one gospel of a resurrected Christ, and another of a new-born spring and budding trees? Is the Christian message that God redeems man, and also that man redeems man?"

"What *do* we Congregationalists believe?" they cry. "What is our Gospel-message to the Twentieth Century world? *Has* our freedom betrayed us, after all? Have we come to the point of simply believing anything we want?"

This whole question of the theology of American Congregationalism is one that has increasingly troubled many of our people. Especially to the younger ministers it has seemed that there should be some great affirmation which we could all make together. They wonder if our freedom was ever intended to mean that we were free to believe anything we wished.

The people at Scrooby and later the men at Savoy were not asking freedom to have *no* standards of belief. They did not want freedom to believe just *anything*. They were asking for freedom of polity; freedom to organize and live as congregations. Their actual theology, their beliefs about

God, and Christ, and the Holy Spirit, and about prayer, and salvation, were practically identical with that of the Presbyterians and not so very different even from the Anglicans. The Savoy Declaration makes it very clear that these Congregationalists considered themselves utterly orthodox and wanted to be recognized—at least by their Presbyterian friends—as being fellow Christians who shared the same convictions of faith.

Their protest was that the Anglicans and even the Presbyterians were drawing from that faith conclusions about the organization and government of church life that were not true to the New Testament and therefore unwarranted. Their argument was on the doctrine of the *Church*. When they read the New Testament they saw churches of Jesus Christ springing up wherever people believed in Him and gathered together as two or three in faith. They saw the word Ecclesia, Church, meaning in almost every instance a single, individual, gathered church and not a hierarchical, organized church, or even the universal Church. They read of "the Church of Christ in Rome," "the Church at Corinth," or "the Church in Ephesus." The first-century Christian Church, it was obvious to them, was a fellowship of autonomous, individual churches, self-governed, visited and advised occasionally by Paul or the other Apostles, but bound together only by the common faith that they all held together, and by their common allegiance to the One whom they all knew as Lord of their lives.

Our 17th century forebears saw that the organization of the first-century Church was one of freedom and independence and they wanted that kind of freedom in order to follow the leading of their Lord whom they met in the pages of the Bible. They wanted, under His guidance, to be able

to make of themselves the same kind of vital, believing churches that Rome, Corinth, and Thessalonica had been.

But they had no desire to believe in a *different* Lord from this Lord of the Bible. They were not interested in interpreting the person of this Christ in some new or different way from the New Testament's way. On the contrary, they wanted to be free to know this Christ in exactly the way the first Christians had known Him. They coveted this New Testament faith. They wanted to know the same redeeming power of the Resurrected Lord that Peter, and John of Patmos, and Paul had known. They wanted to be free to obey Him as those first fishermen had obeyed Him. They wanted to receive the same new life that had once been given to Lazarus so long ago.

It was to know Christ that the fathers of Congregationalism wanted to be free. As far as they were concerned, Jesus Christ was the man from Nazareth in whom God Himself had come directly and decisively into the life of the world and the life of men. He was the Christ in whom God was present, "reconciling the World to Himself." He was the King of Kings, and Lord of Lords.

No one at Savoy wanted to change that. They had as "high" a view of Christ as any Anglican or Presbyterian— perhaps higher, in view of their willingness to live a denominational life that would depend utterly for authority upon the leading of His Spirit. The saints at Savoy were deeply concerned about theology—concerned that the great truths of the Christian faith be preserved among them in all their New Testament power.

Certainly, there was no doubt among them that there *were* great truths of faith on which all Congregationalists— indeed all Christians—could agree. And it is this that has troubled so many in American Congregationalism today: that there should be among us such wide diversity and even disagreement on the essential beliefs of the faith.

These people want terribly to find what the great truths are among us and to encourage us to stand for them. Many are deeply influenced by the "sterner theology" of the great European theologians of the Reformed tradition—particularly in reaction to the liberal, even Unitarian tendencies among us. They want to shore up what they believe is our failing theological integrity. And in their enthusiasm, the idea of a denominational creed and an accepted theology looks awfully good. Creeds and confessions have often seemed a tempting way to strengthen faith, and do so now, as many look forward to a united Church.

And in a sense they are right. We *must* discover what our faith is! But not at the price of legalism; for no church has ever won a great faith by legislation and law.

Somewhere there is an historic and continuing faith that men and women of the Congregational Way have held dear through all the changes of thought and adventures of life of our three hundred years. My own hope and prayer is that, as a whole people, we may be led by our Lord to find it.

We have spoken already of our "covenant" relation in Congregationalism, and of our "freedom." But in both cases it was a covenant with one Jesus of Nazareth and a freedom in the Spirit that was bound by a love for Him. If anything is true in all of this, it is that our faith and our very way of life depends somehow upon our understanding of that one dominating figure of Christian history whose span of years on earth are measured from a stable in Nazareth to a cross outside Jerusalem.

The apostle Paul, who knew the Christian Gospel if any-one did, believed with all his heart and preached to every congregation he ever faced "that Jesus Christ is Lord"—that it was through Christ, and Him alone, that men can become Christians and know God in His fulness. It seems to me, therefore, that it is through this Christ that we, like our forefathers, should seek to understand our faith.

One question we should ask is what the *first* Congregationalists believed. What was *their* theology? What did they think about God, and Christ, and the Holy Spirit? What was their conviction about salvation, about heaven and hell, and about eternal life? Was Jesus the supreme man of earth? Was the Holy Spirit just the light of knowledge in the heart of a man? Was heaven an ideal and hell a fiction? Would some men really be saved and some not? Where did those saints of the seventeenth century take their stand?

The Declaration of Faith which they made at Savoy leaves little doubt. God for them was "the alone Fountain" of faith and known to them in three ways, "which Doctrine of the Trinity" they said, "is the foundation of all our communion with God, and comfortable dependence upon Him." [1] Christ they called the Mediator, the one who came "in his Humane nature, . . . united to the Divine . . . and underwent the punishment due to us . . . being made sin and a curse for us . . ." [2] They believed also that "Whereas there is none that doth good, and sinneth not . . . God hath in the covenant of grace mercifully provided, that Believers so sinning and falling, be renewed through repentance unto Salvation." [3]

[1] End of Section 3 of Savoy Declaration of Faith.
[2] In Section 8, ibid.
[3] In number 2 of Section 15, ibid.

And ultimately their faith looked toward the final day in the conviction that "the Bodies of men after death return to dust, and see corruption, but their souls (which neither die nor sleep) . . . immediately return to God who gave them, the souls of the righteous being then made perfect in holiness, and received into the highest Heavens, where they behold the face of God in light and glory . . . and the souls of the wicked are cast into Hell, where they remain in torment and darkness, reserved to the Judgment of the great day . . ." [4]

They did not perhaps express their faith just as we might express it. Indeed, they were more honest than we in facing the real implications of faith. Some of us would surely find it awkward to speak quite so plainly about Judgment. And yet, what is so completely obvious to anyone who reads through the Savoy Declaration is that those men lived by a powerful faith: that Jesus Christ was at the heart of that faith; that they felt God Himself to be revealed in that Nazarene's life; and that they took this Christ seriously. He came to save men, saying to them, "Come, follow Me" —and those who did follow *were* saved, and those who turned their backs on Christ were lost. These men really believed Christ was the Saviour of the World. They really believed that He gave men a choice—a terrible, wonderful, eternal choice. And they knew that Death would not be the end, and that some day, somewhere, man would be judged!

Their faith was in some parts brittle and arbitrary, perhaps. But it was also vital and living; a profound conviction that He whom the New Testament presented to all men was indeed the Lord of all men—a Lord to be loved, and obeyed, and followed.

[4] From article 1 of section 31, ibid.

It was the Christ of the New Testament that the 17th century founders of Congregationalism wanted. And they believed that He could be found in the New Testament, and that the New Testament alone proclaimed Him in His fulness and alone set forth the kind of Christian community in which He wanted His disciples to live. The apostolic church, therefore, was an ideal for them—a way of life to be emulated, a free, creative fellowship to be recovered.

This is why they called upon their sovereign and her government "to bring home the people of God to the purity and truth of the Apostolic Church." [5] And if she would not do it, they were ready to do it themselves. As William Bradford wrote in his history of the Pilgrims, their objection was to "ye lordly and tyrannous power of ye prelates" and their "unlawful and anti-Christian . . . offices . . . and courts and canons," for the one reason that they had "no warrant in ye word of God."

Obviously, what they wanted was to return, through the evidence of the Bible, to the church-life and faith of the Apostolic Church. The truth of the Gospel was to be found, they insisted, right there in the New Testament itself, and in its record of the apostle's preaching and teaching.

"But who is to say what the truth of the Bible *is?*" some will almost certainly protest. "Don't say that *you* are going to tell us what the Bible *really* says! The Bible has meaning only as each man interprets it. There are many interpretations, and you can only give yours!"

Now I grant this. There is a sense in which this is quite true. There have been different interpretations of what the

[5] Quoted in Atkins and Fagley, *History of American Congregationalism,* p. 31.

essential New Testament Gospel is. Some have immersed themselves in the immortal Sermon on the Mount and proclaimed Jesus as the greatest of teachers. Their cry is, "the teachings and ethics of Jesus are the thing!" Some have seen the social implications of His teachings and made Him a reformer of society. Others have emphasized Jesus' ministry as a healer.

Some say He was a man—the greatest of men—but only a man. But there are others who have proclaimed Him as more than a man, as Son of God *and* Son of Man, He in Whom God Himself came into the world to redeem the world from sin and despair.

Is there, in all this, some one, central, and overwhelming conviction which the Apostolic Church believed and proclaimed above all others, and which the first Congregationalists accepted as the truth of the Gospel? I think there is. And I think that we who make bold to use for ourselves this name which our seventeenth-century forebears suffered to hand on to us, are under peculiar obligation to weigh very carefully their convictions about the faith before we too quickly discard them. This great conviction of the early Congregationalists accepts and rejoices in the teachings, the ethics, and the example of Jesus' life. But it says that something even more wonderful was happening. It says that "God was in Christ, reconciling the world to Himself."

Some moderns say Jesus was too humble to proclaim Himself, or to make Himself equal with God. But listen to His own words. There was a day before the Jews when He said: "I and my Father are one" (John 10:30). They called it blasphemy, and took up stones to stone Him, but He never recanted.

He said also: "He that believeth on Me, believeth not on

Me but on Him that sent Me" (John 12:44). At the Last Supper, when He had washed His disciples' feet and sat down, He said, "Ye call Me Master and Lord: and ye say well; for so I am" (John 13:13).

And in Mark's account of the Gospel, when Jesus had been standing in silence before the Sanhedrin, the high priest finally asked the fatal question: "Art Thou the Christ, the Son of the Blessed?" And Jesus answered: "I am: and ye shall see the Son of Man sitting on the right hand of power, and coming in the clouds of heaven!" That was when the high priest tore his clothes and cried: "What need ye any further witnesses? Ye have heard the blasphemy; what think ye?" And they all condemned Him to be guilty of death—because He had committed the unpardonable sin of making Himself more than a man, and claiming equality with God!

Was it such a very different Gospel from this, as some say it was, when the young Church of the apostles centered its message on Christ himself—and not on Him as teacher, or prophet, or saint, but as risen, redeeming Lord? The first sermon Peter ever preached, recorded in the second chapter of Acts, says this:

"Ye men of Israel, hear these words: Jesus of Nazareth, a man approved of God among you by miracles and wonders and signs . . . which God did by Him in the midst of you, as ye yourselves also know . . . God hath made that same Jesus Whom ye crucified, both Lord and Christ . . . Therefore repent, and be baptized every one of you in the name of Jesus Christ, for the remission of sins."

This was the "Good News" those first Christians were spreading everywhere. Peter preached it; Stephen preached it; Paul preached it. Jesus' ethics, and teachings, and example of life will stand forever as a guide and inspiration to Christian men, and indeed, to all men. But for the first-century Church they were not *the Gospel.* The "Good News" for them, the "Good News" which meant forgiveness and new life to that Roman world, was that "God so loved the world that He gave His only begotten Son, that all who believe in Him should not perish, but have everlasting life."

According to all the evidences we have, our Congregational fathers of the seventeenth century were convinced with Saint Paul and the Church of the first century that Jesus Christ is not prophet, saint, or teacher—but *Lord!*

We have an idea then, of what the First Congregationalists believed. It was a Bible-faith, an attempt to capture for their own hearts what the great Christians of Apostolic times had believed. And their faith centered in the person of Christ—the Christ Who was Son of God and Saviour of the World.

But how was this figure of history all these things? Our Congregational fathers insisted that their faith was what they called "Trinitarian": "Which doctrine of the Trinity," they said, "is the foundation of all our Communion with God . . ." [6] And Congregationalists today, for all their apparent differences of theology, *still* claim to be Trinitarian in their belief about Christ. What do we mean by this word? What is the doctrine of the Trinity, and how can it fit into our faith today?

Our belief in the Trinity is the keystone of Christian

[6] As quoted earlier from the Savoy Declaration of Faith.

faith. Yet it is the very thing that poses a serious problem for many people: the one stumbling block in the doorway that prevents them from embracing a full Christian faith.

From those outside the Church who would believe if only this doctrine were not such an affront to their intelligence, the exasperated out-cry comes: "Why must you insist on your strange formula of three persons, yet one God? How can you expect a reasonable man to believe that? Give us a simple faith of striving for goodness, love of one's neighbor, and concern for the unfortunate. But don't make us swallow this impossible creed!"

Even by those within the Church the perplexed remark is sometimes made: "I believe in Christ as the Son of God, but don't ask me to understand the mysteries of the doctrine of the Trinity—that is the job of theologians, not of ordinary Christians like us."

How misunderstood, this core of our faith! How slow we are to see that this doctrine was never intended to be an exercise of the mind, but an experience of the heart! We must understand this before anything else: the Christian doctrine of the Trinity does not come to us from the pen of some first-century scholar who conceived it out of intellectual wrestlings in a secluded library or quiet study. It is no mere doctrinal point in an arid theology. It springs from the deep wells of human experience. It is what men like you and me discovered by their own experience to be true about God.

They couldn't explain it. Read any of the countless efforts of the Church to explain the Trinity in a few words. It is always an inadequate and unsatisfactory attempt. Words have never been able to say it, but faith has always known it to be true. No one believed more strongly in one

God than did the early Christians. But after knowing Jesus, the carpenter from Nazareth, and then discovering beyond Easter His invisible but powerful presence among them still, they found they just had to speak of God not only as the Father Who had created the heavens and the earth, but also as the Son who had dwelt among them, and finally as the Holy Spirit Who still was with them! Only then could they begin to say all that they felt and meant by the word God.

They were not trying to write theology. They were merely spreading the good news about a God Who had come to them in a way they had never dreamed possible.

God, to those early Christians, was the one Lord of Heaven and earth Whom Israel had always worshipped. The God of their faith was He Who touched the darkness with the dawn on creation's first day as "the morning stars sang together and the sons of God shouted for joy." He was the One Who said, "Let there be light," and there was light; Who made the earth and Who fashioned from its dust the first man; Who chose Israel for His own, and Who led her from Egypt to Canaan and made her a people.

Their God was the One who loved His people Israel as His own child and Who had cried out to her again and again through the prophets, seeking to win her back as she repeatedly turned away from Him. He was the God Who refused to be defeated in His central purpose in history of bringing all men to Him. To them the very fulfillment of this purpose was that the God of creation had finally clothed with flesh the Word He had been speaking through the prophets and had actually come among men *in a man* to cry out that same word in a new way.

The early Christians never lost their faith in this one

true God, Creator of heaven and earth, and Father of all the children of men. This conviction was secure with them. Nor did they ever set about to devise theological systems or to dream up anything called the doctrine of the Trinity.

What happened to them was an *experience* of God. This God, Whom those men had been worshipping in synagogue and temple from childhood, they suddenly found one day to be confronting them in a man! It was a strange thing: one moment mending nets on the Galilean Sea, and the next moment answering the call of a total stranger who said, "Come, follow me, and I will make you fishers of men."

That was the way it began for Andrew and Peter, James and John. And with each day the conviction grew that somehow this man was *more* than a man. Fully a man, yes. A man who told them how He had been tempted in the desert; a man Who wept over Lazarus; a man Who, on their long walks grew tired even as they were tired; indeed, a man who even seemed to hunger for friendship as they themselves did.

And yet they felt something in Him that they had never seen in another man. Something that they knew in their hearts did not exist in any other man. This man was without sin. They had never lived in the presence of such goodness before. It was a goodness that seemed always to be reaching out toward other men in love and in healing power. This man also possessed a strange authority. His disciples could tell that even the scribes and pharisees, who were hostile to Him, recognized His authority. Moreover, this man possessed power—not only power to heal the sick and raise the dead—but power to make men good; power to make them want to be better than they had ever been before; power to give such a profound new meaning to their lives that it came as new life itself.

As time passed, the conviction grew on that band of twelve that the very God of heaven and earth Whom they had always known had, in a strange way, come among them in this man Jesus. When he spoke to them some word of judgment it seemed as if God Himself were speaking, and when He looked at them in love it seemed that the eyes of God were upon them.

How could they say it? How could they explain what they felt? They said it, each one, as their hearts told them to say it. For Peter it came as a blurted confession on that day when Jesus asked "Whom say ye that I am?"—"Thou art the Christ, the Son of the Living God!" For John, the writer of the Gospel, it came as the tremendous assertion that this Jesus was the Word of God—the Word that many times through prophets and priests had been spoken and now had come itself as a man: "In the beginning was the Word, and the Word was with God, and the Word was God!" Word of God, Son of God—however they said it they meant the truth the Christian world has come to believe, that "God was in Christ, reconciling the world to Himself."

But probably strangest of all was what happened after Christ died. That terrible death on a cross could have finished everything for those Christians. To whom would they go? God had never been so real to them as He had been in Jesus. And yet curiously, it was only after Jesus' death and resurrection that they even *began* to know the depths of God. For at Pentecost He revealed Himself to them in yet a third way.

Jesus had said on the night of the last supper, "I will

pray the Father, and He shall give you another Comforter . . . Which is the Holy Spirit . . . and He shall teach you all things . . ." It was on the day of Pentecost that God came to them again—not as Creator-God and Father, and not as divine and human son, but as the Spirit. It was another Person of the same God Who over-powered them that day; a Person Who came upon them like wind, invisible, yet an inspirer and giver of Power, that not even the Father and the Son had been.

He it was Who sent them out from Jerusalem into all the world to preach the Gospel. He it was Who raised up Christians in Antioch, Corinth, Thessalonica, and Rome. He it was Who gathered the young church together and fashioned it into an inspired column for Christ.

This Person of power was God, and yet not the same as God had been known to them as Creator or Christ. He was the Spirit: God the Holy Spirit. How else could they say it? How else could Paul bless his friends in Corinth but with "The grace of the Lord Jesus Christ, and the love of God, and the communion of the Holy Spirit be with you all!"

No wonder the Church of Christ as it grew tried to find ways of telling this wonderful truth that meant the world to them. No wonder the Church speaks with stumbling words of the doctrine of the Trinity. One God in three Persons—that was the faith of the early Church, and that has been the faith of the whole church since: not just an idea, but a very wonderful reality of Christian experience.

Christ was Himself the heart of that experience: Christ in Whom God split history asunder, opening to men the depths of His love. It was through these "unsearchable riches of Christ" that His followers in all ages have found

God as Father, Spirit, Son. This is why they were able to confess that, for them, "Jesus is Lord!"

There it was, a simple yet rock-bound faith, fashioned by experience. No scholars' dream, no fantasy of the mind, no brittle and unbending creed—but a living, precious encounter with a life: *God's* life; one three-personed God.

This faith is believable! It was the apostle's faith. It was the faith of our Congregational fathers. And we claim it for our faith. This is the Trinity: Not a fanciful, but a winsome, winning thing.

And yet we must confess that the pendulum of history has swung wide in our Congregational Way. This living faith of the early Church which inspired our seventeenth-century forebears tended, as time passed, to become encumbered with a dogmatism that at times cursed Congregationalism with a spirit of legalism and intolerance.

More than once logic got the better of them. More than once the love of a redeeming Lord Who came to save sinners and not to damn them seems to have been forgotten. The saintly spirit, devout faith, and passion for freedom of a man like Pastor Robinson was not always emulated by his descendants in the faith. The uncharitable legalisms and narrow spirit of some Congregationalists seemed to grow from a misuse of the doctrine of double predestination—a feeling that some men were quite arbitrarily fore-doomed to be lost and others to be saved: a conviction that tempted many to speculate on who the damned were and to publicly treat them accordingly.

Thus some people were considered to be heretics and therefore rightly to be ostracized. In some parts of New

England, witches were hanged, and Quakers persecuted. Perhaps we can hardly blame those who left for Rhode Island seeking a tolerance not always found in Massachusetts.

It was close to inevitable that among these New England Congregationalists, who seemed to thrive on the logic and controversy of speculative theology, a reaction would be produced toward a more liberal and humane spirit. Aided by the growing ferment and tolerance of new ideas brought by Deism and Arminianism at the time of the Revolutionary War, such a movement did grow within Congregationalism and culminated in the crisis known as the "Unitarian Departure" in 1825.

Unitarianism was at that time essentially a freeing movement that prepared the way for the liberal theology which later blossomed within the Congregationalism of mid-nineteenth century New England. Two important forces influenced this growth of liberalism. One was the new science; the other was Biblical criticism which brought history, science, and archaeology to bear upon our understanding of the Bible.

From a rather strict dogmatism, the swing was now toward a liberalism that was to become, in some cases, more a philosophy than a faith. Liberalism made its peace with both of these scientific and intellectual movements.

But it went too far. It won great freedoms, but it began to lose its grip on the essential gospel. Its respect for science and its doubts about the Bible made its faith more and more a man-centered thing, until finally it was proclaiming less and less the redeeming power of a risen Christ, and more and more the mere teaching and leadership of a Jesus Who was simply and only a man. It became a gospel of social progress, aiming for a "kingdom of God" with which God had less to do than almighty man who would win it by himself.

Because it was free, the swings and splits in Congregationalism never brought a "heresy" trial, because no one had the right to try anyone else. It is to our credit that we did not shut our eyes to the insights of science, as some did; that we were open enough to accept scholarship's criticism of the Bible; that our Way has become characterized by a passion for social justice. The result is one of the finest traditions of Biblical and theological scholarship in American Protestantism, perhaps its best-educated ministry, and certainly one of its freest spirits of fellowship and tolerance.

But we took our freedom so far that thousands of Congregationalists no longer know what they believe. They no longer have a Gospel to sustain them in the tensions and terrors of a century far different from the days when an easy optimism flourished.

Where then, does this leave us? Where does this leave all of Congregationalism in our search to discover what we believe—what the great faith *is* of "the Congregational Way?"

For one thing, the tide of reaction to our liberalism has been running now for thirty years. The pendulum is swinging back toward orthodoxy. But must it also swing back to a new dogmatism and intolerance?

It could! The possibility is there. The danger is real. One senses in our decade a new intolerance for minority positions, one hears with shame the groans and laughter that greet some men who hold unpopular opinions when they stand up in the great councils of our fellowship, and one notes with sorrow the yearning of so many for a "firmer theology" and a required creed of faith to fling at the world.

It is not meanness or narrowness. It is an honest yearning and a sincere impatience for Congregationalism to stand for something! They want us to have the power, as a people, which the discipline of high standards can give. They want us to have a faith we can believe, and glory in, and proclaim to all the world together.

But the danger is that they want to capture that faith in a creed and a law that will preserve it pure and undefiled. That will be the only way left unless we ordinary people of the churches can first capture it in our hearts, and make it live again with power in our lives!

Where can we find such a faith to agree upon? In Reformation days, the first Congregationalists went straight to the New Testament and found it in the by-ways of Galilee, in an upper room at Jerusalem, at the foot of a cross, and on the highroads of an empire where a Paul, and a Peter, and a Barnabus walked. *That* is where they found the true and eternal Gospel. That is the only place where we can find it, and where we can learn the truth about the Lord of life Who is alive and at work today.

And it *can* be found if we have the courage, and the love, and the perseverance to walk those roads again through the pages of our Bibles. For this is the Book which our fathers intended to be the guide of our Way. Because only here can we meet our Christ; only here can we meet Him in all His fulness and know in our hearts the Truth that "Jesus is Lord!"

This is our creed, this our confession of faith. And if we can believe this with our whole hearts, and know through His Book of books His will for us, we need never be ashamed of being known as people of the Congregational Way.

5. "Life in the Gathered Church"

There is not a Christian Church in America which does not have its own peculiar characteristics. No matter what its denomination, no matter on what street corner it stands —every church has a reputation. It is the "social" church or the "serious" church. It is the "influential" church or the "small" church. It is the "live" or the "dead" church. It may be friendly, or it may be cold: but people know. In a thousand subtle ways, people know.

But what *should* it be? What is the Christian Church *here* to be? What should characterize its life—its activities, its work in the world, the witness of its members? And quite specifically, as Christians of the Congregational Way, what should be unique about the life of *our* Churches? Have we a vision burning in our souls of some special witness we can make?

In the third chapter of the first book of Samuel there is an interesting and important sentence: "And the Word of the Lord was rare in those days: there was no frequent vision." Perhaps this says something about the Christian

Church today. For there could be no more devastating tragedy in the life of the Church than this. The poet, the artist, and the writer depend for their very existence upon the creative inspiration that comes to them from beyond themselves. So also the Church depends for its life upon the frequent revelation of God's Word to His people, and upon the continual invasion into their midst of the Holy Spirit.

It was the very charter of the Church that "your young men shall see visions, and your old men shall dream dreams." For a community like the Church, whose life is in heaven as well as upon earth, this is an absolute necessity. Indeed the Church of Christ was born amid the strange happenings of Pentecost. This was the baptism of the Spirit through which the Church for centuries to come would be enabled to hear God's Word and to see His will for His people.

Christians have always insisted that they did not walk alone in the world, that somehow, whatever difficulty might arise, God would have some word for them of guidance and of help. As Pastor John Robinson told the Mayflower pilgrims, "The Lord hath yet more truth and light to break forth from His Holy Word." The very essence of life for the man of faith, is to believe that, going before him through every hour of his life, is the "cloud by day" and the "pillar of fire by night."

It is not difficult to imagine then, what a disaster it must have been for Israel in the time of Samuel, that "the Word of the Lord was rare in those days," that "there was no frequent vision." Their one source of inspiration and hope dried up like a spring freshet in the baking heat of midsummer: no men with prophet's eyes to scan the landscape of eternity; no still small voice to add assuring splendor to their hours of prayer. It must have seemed as though heaven itself had ceased to speak, and had closed its ears to their cry forever!

The one people who expected and longed for this contact with the Divine, suddenly found themselves living in darkness and silence before their God. A kind of spiritual drought had fallen across the face of the land. This was disaster indeed for the children of Israel.

But for a people in the mid-twentieth century, whose eyes are not accustomed to seeing visions, nor whose ears are used to listening for a word from heaven, it is no less a disaster when visions fade and the voice of God is no longer heard in the land. Because in our time such blindness and deafness to the face and Word of God is to cut ourselves off from the very source and power of our life. The Church of today is too often unaware even of the existence of visions it has never seen, and of the voice it has never heard.

To our loss it is no longer the custom in the Church of today for congregations to gather of a Sunday morning in trembling and silent awe at the prospect of standing revealed and unprotected in the holy presence of God. It is not the custom for the Lord's people to demand of their preacher, "Sir, we would see Jesus!" and really believe that by God's mercy he can show them the Master's face. It is not the custom for modern Christians to keep lone vigils of prayer, or to pore for hours over the mysteries of the Bible. It is not the custom for our "young men to see visions" and our "old men to dream dreams."

In our busy world the people of God have little time for such things. These are too embarrassing, too pious. The Church talks of statistical gains instead of the glory of God in its midst. It builds up thousands of sanctuaries and classroom additions but not thousands of broken and demolished lives. It says to its sick and dying, "We are *thinking* of you," but rarely "We are praying for your deliverance from disease and death." It issues judgments innumerable on the state of society, but does not hear the judgment of God upon the state of its own soul.

It can be said just as truly of the Christian Church today that "the Word of the Lord is rare" in *these* days; and among *us* "there is no frequent vision."

Surely this is a sign that something has gone wrong in the modern Church. It may not be the immorality which was the problem in Samuel's day, it may not be any glaring evil. But might it not be that Christian churches have on every hand capitulated, completely or in part, to the forces of secular life around them?

I wonder if the booming, bizarre success of the super-markets and the shopping-centers, the fund-raisers and the advertisers, the television shows and the out-door movies haven't worked a subtle deviltry in the heart of the Church. Once the Church rejoiced over "two or three" meeting in the secret glow of the brothers of "the Way." Once she saw her task as first growing in faith and then preaching the Gospel to the world. Once she cared more about the one sinner saved than the ninety-nine hangers-on who might pad the roll for the yearbook records.

But today it is the "Big Show" that counts. Not so much the thronged meetings, so easily and so readily criticized, where a great evangelist may reap for Christ the harvest we failed to reap, but more particularly the worked-up, pressure-built extravaganzas which leaders in all denominations love to bill as a "great witness of Protestant strength!" Things have got to be big for us today, and successful.

"How many came?" is the question. Meetings of women, meetings of men, meetings of young people—that's what we want. Locally, it is the church that can put on a supper with a high tab and wide enough appeal to pack the dining room to the doors that is considered "alive." The bazaar that nets a few thousand is another one of today's sure signs of church success. And of course the biggest show yet is the building project ably managed by the outside professionals who promise success not only in stone and steel, but also in larger numbers, increased attendance, and that all-important "spiritual factor" whose astonishing rise can be plotted by a green line on a graph—in advance, if you please!

All the techniques of advertising, all the efficiency of modern business, all the manipulations of the mass communicators are the word in the Church today. It is not the Joneses, but the "times" that we must keep up with, they tell us. The Church must be made appealing, it must be as exciting and entertaining as the world around it, and in the same way. Until, in our effort to attract the world to our doors, we have become like the world—with no new life to offer and no word of judgment and hope to speak.

We have been trying to live as if there were no difference between the Church and the world: as if the work of the Church was just one more activity in our lives, and not in itself a whole new way of life. Christian churches today by the hundreds have become mere social institutions in the minds of their people.

We haven't *expected* our life in the fellowship of believers to be transforming; we haven't *expected* in the hour of worship to hear God's Word of Judgment spoken against us; we haven't *expected* to be commissioned by this Christ to preach the Gospel to the poor and to heal the broken-hearted; we haven't *expected* great things—the *really* great things—to happen.

And so the great things have not happened. The Church has not been a community of reborn men, thrilling to the wonder of the Resurrection-discovery. It has not stood in the market-place of life and shouted the victory-cry: "I know that my Redeemer liveth!"

This means that the Church has not truly been the Church, and so it is little wonder that in our time, just as in Samuel's time, the Word of the Lord has been rare, and there has been "no frequent vision."

It is this situation in our churches that we are here to change. God does not ask us to go out and change the whole Church. Instead, He has given to each one of us our own church, the church in our town, the church we know and love. This is the church He gives us, and with it He gives the power, through faith, to work miracles within its life.

But the miracles of transformation will be wrought only through those who have a vision of what God means the Church to be. And for those of us who are Christians of the Congregational Way there ought to be a very special vision.

Congregational churches have traditionally thought of themselves as "gathered" churches: churches "gathered" around Jesus Christ with His Spirit in the midst. If this is a valid concept of church life; if all we have been saying about freedom, and about being a covenant people, and about accepting Jesus as absolute Lord of our lives, with no ecclesiastical machinery in between, is true; then there must be a quite particular kind of life which is ours to live. "Life in the gathered church."

This life in the gathered church is first of all the utterly personal life of the whole people. Before it ever gets to what goes on in the church, it is what goes on in the life of each individual member that counts.

This is important in any church, but it is crucial in a Congregational church. Because with us the church *is* the people. It is not the minister and not the denomination, but the people themselves. The power, the witness, the work of any given church stands or falls with what the people are.

In our "Way" there is no reprieve, no second line of defense, no reinforcements from a higher echelon. We stand alone. The success of every venture depends completely upon the members. No one else is going to cover for us. It is our responsibility.

The very word "Congregational" shows where our emphasis lies. Our belief is in the priesthood of *all* believers— never in the priesthood of just the minister alone. We are priests and ministers to each other. We are the ones who are called to care for the brethren, to feed the hungry, to clothe the naked, to heal the sick, and to preach the coming of the Kingdom. A Congregational church is the *people's* church. It *belongs* to them. It is *their* work, *their* life, *their* responsibility.

There may be no one who can tell them what to do. But woe be unto them if they have not a zeal in their own hearts that tells them what they *must* do! The people are the ones who must have the visions, who must seek the Spirits' guidance, and who must lead the way, and give themselves to the going of God's work; for no one will do it for them.

This is the whole meaning of the Church Meeting: that the people gather together in prayer to do the church's work; that they refuse to cast the burden solely upon a few directors or trustees, and that they come to be led together into a new way.

This seems to be terribly hard for lay people to see. They sense it as a burden, as something they pay a minister to do *for* them. He looms in their minds as a specialist, a trained mind and man all prepared to do the work of prayer. "*I —pray* with someone grieved or sick?" a layman asks. "Don't be ridiculous. I wouldn't presume!"

They forget that the great preachers and pray-ers of the New Testament Church were all laymen. Those first-century Christians ministered to men because God called them to do it, because this is what they believed Christians were *supposed* to do. They didn't sit around with downcast gaze because they hadn't been to theological seminary. They marched! A motley company of fishermen, farmers, harlots, and tax-collectors, they marched. They knew that words would be given them, and power would be poured out. This was their Church, the Church of Christ the Lord, and they were determined to make her great. Jesus had said they would do greater works than He and in a sense they did. They healed and they helped, they sang and they preached the Kingdom, because they knew that they were the ones who had been called and that they were themselves the bearers of the trust.

Ministers came too. There was a place for them. They were needed. But it was the conviction of the early Congregationalists, as it seems certainly to have been of the early Christians, that a minister was set aside only to do full time the same things that the people of the church were to do part time. Not a difference in function, but a difference in time.

It is the lay people then, who carry on the church's ministry, who preach in their lives the Gospel, who have a care for souls, and who—especially as deacons—serve as under-shepherds of the flock, along with the minister. It is the people themselves whose responsibility is the Church.

What better reason for the first element of life in the gathered church being that of a disciplined devotional life on the part of all the members? If "the people" of a church which depends so completely on its members, have no personal life of prayer and devotion, then this kind of responsibility can only become demonic in their hands. For then they are trying to do a job they are completely incompetent to do, and inevitably they will begin to do it for the wrong reasons and the wrong ends. What happens most usually is that they begin to run their church as a business, begin to evaluate its success by business standards, and all too soon begin to make it an institution swallowed up by the ideals and practices of the world—an institution bereft of the mighty Word it was sent to speak and shorn of the power with which to speak it.

The Church of Jesus Christ is not a business, but a mission. And if that part of it called Congregational is to *be* Congregational its people are under a double obligation to be people of prayer.

Perhaps the most obvious place to begin is in the worshipping community. If a Christian is not part of the church when it gathers for worship, he is just not part of the church. This is where the "gathered church," yea, any church, lives. So a Christian of the Congregational Way is under special obligation to be at worship each week. But the nourishment of a Christian life needs much more than this. After all, we are at worship in church only an hour a week. The vast majority of our hours are spent at home and at work. How can we be growing in faith there?

Certainly a minimum prayer-life in every home is grace at meals. Here we can give thanks to God for the gift of food which He gives most of us in such over-flowing measure. This is the least embarrassing act of personal devotion, and if a family makes a habit of never forgetting it—not even in public—they will be the stronger for it.

Most essential after this minimum is achieved, is a time of private prayer. The best time for this is usually in the morning before breakfast, when thoughts are clear and the mind and heart can take in all the concerns, all the hopes and fears, all the people and duties of the coming day and offer them up to God. Fifteen or twenty minutes of such a "morning watch" filled with adoration, thanksgiving, asking, intercession, dedication, and just plain listening will soon become a source of tremendous power and serenity in the life of the believer. Preceding the "morning watch" might come a time of Bible reading. Even a Bible in the kitchen or on the family book-shelf where it can be read in snatches of time is a great help. But it should be read. Indeed, it must be if we are to hear God's Word to us and make most creative use of our prayer time.

Short prayers can be breathed at any moment and for some, perhaps, every moment of the day. Family prayers with or without scripture reading should be a goal to be worked toward and achieved as soon as all members can accept it gladly. And finally, when evening comes all men do well in thought and prayer to give their lives back to God for His keeping through the night.

The practices of prayer vary in a thousand ways and each of us must choose his own. Do not worry over-much about which one you use. Just be sure you do *have* one, and practice it as faithfully, as you honestly can. This is when the Christian life will begin to mean something. And this is also when churches of the Congregational Way will begin to practice the first great requirement of "life in the church."

A second characteristic of this "life" is a certain spirit about its people—an attitude of mind and heart, an air of expectancy, a sense of adventure.

Our forefathers of the Puritan stream, which came to Massachusetts Bay, had it. They came determined to work out the Puritan pattern of life as an example to the world and especially to their persecutors in England. Their cry was "We are as a city that is set upon a hill, and the eyes of the world are upon us!" For them, it was a great adventure, an exciting new experiment in Christian life.

Only if we modern Congregationalists of America, too, have this spirit in our hearts can our way of Church life be turned back toward the creative and powerful thing our fathers intended it to be. The essence of Congregationalism, depending as it does on a seeking people and a leading Christ, should certainly be a spirit of open eagerness—as if the Master were continually thundering in our hearts: "Look up, lift up your heads; for your redemption draweth nigh!"

Men who are constantly expecting the great things of God to happen in their midst will never be without this eager, hopeful gaze. Their hearts will continually thrill to the singing joy of John of Patmos who could cry: "Behold, I saw a new heaven and a new earth!" This is what all of us must be expecting in the midst of our churches: "A new heaven and a new earth."

If Christ is truly in our midst then we will not be exhausting our energies in food sales and bazaars, socials and suppers—good enough in their places, but with too great priority in most of our churches. We will be looking for the great events of faith in our midst. We will sense a leading of the Spirit. People will come into our churches and know immediately in their hearts: "Something is here. These people *have* something—a quality, a power, a passion, and a depth!"

It will be in everything we do. It might even mean that there would be no more of those awful, ambling, Godless committee meetings among us. Perhaps those meetings would be begun in prayer, and ended in prayer—and not the minister's prayers, either!

A group like the Board of Deacons might find itself transformed from the essentially honorary row of pillars which most of our churches know, into a working, praying, serving corps of fellow pastors with the minister, as they most certainly were in the early Church and are today in traditions like that of the Presbyterian Church of Scotland. Think of all that their hearts might find to do in a church so touched by the Spirit: regular meetings with the minister to share in the great concerns of their church; an hour of study at those meetings to prepare themselves spiritually to be better deacons and better Christians; calling upon certain families where the minister feels that the word and the hand of a dedicated Deacon might help and heal;

personal growth in prayer so that they in turn might help others to grow in prayer; eyes and hearts made perhaps a little keener to see the great opportunities for evangelism and mission in the community and beyond it, and the courage and faith to inspire the minister and the people to attempt the task that God may seem so surely to be putting before them.

All these and a host of other exciting developments might come from the touch of God upon the lives of such spiritual leaders in a Congregational church. For again, it is *their* church, and they too are priests and ministers with their pastors. All of us, if we seriously want this, would do well to return to the practice commended at Savoy, of actually ordaining deacons by the laying on of hands and by prayer. They could not help but sense then, the high calling and work before them.

Other things, too, would take place in a church sincerely "gathered" around Christ and desiring to be led by Him. Individual lives would be changed. Men and women would begin to know the apostolic joy that could sing: "I live, yet it is not I who live, but Christ Who liveth in me!" and the whole congregation would begin to feel this stirring. Hearts and minds would rouse up and the excitement would pass from life to life until the demand might be made for opportunity to meet as Christian friends to read the Bible, or to pray, or to study new depths of the faith. Small groups might begin to meet to pray for the church itself and to carry on their hearts the pastor as he goes his rounds, to remember the sick of the parish in their suffering, to bear up the sorrowing for comfort at the throne of grace. Others might meet to read the Bible and to learn the treasures that they never knew were there.

Groups long established in the church might find themselves lifted above the traditional horizons too often binding them, to see daringly new possibilities for their endeavors. Men's Clubs might stop fleeing the specter of "Religion" and turn and do battle with the beast by seeking to learn something about it through planned discussions among their own members. They might look for a real Christian mission of friendship and service in their area which they could make their own.

Young people might find their idealism challenged to set themselves a course of prayer, or to make themselves a missionary task force in some special need in their community's life, or perhaps to sincerely educate themselves for more intelligent Christian citizenship. They might even find themselves led into fearless study of the great issues of the day from a Christian perspective, and into a decision to do something about them.

These are things which do not happen as a result of suggestions or planned programs from higher quarters. They happen when the minds and hearts of individual people in a gathered congregation are kindled, and when their fire lights other fires until the spirits of hundreds are aflame with the Gospel! It is in the openness of a community not bound by law but by the Spirit, where this can happen. It can happen here because the people are the church, and every person is important and needed. No man's word goes unheeded in such a fellowship if it is truly of Christ. The young and the old, the educated and the poorly-educated, the farmers and the professors—all are heard, for the people of the gathered church know that there is no man among them through whom their Christ would not deign to speak.

The possibilities are unlimited when the Spirit is present.

Creative new forms of fellowship are forever flowering and filling new needs as the hunger of souls deepens and reaches out for the truth.

And by no means need it be purely a selfish thing. Prayer groups and Bible study groups and fellowship groups have a way of turning outside of themselves; out toward the world around them, out toward the needs crying at their doorstep, out toward the lives desperate and lost. Soon enough they learn that theirs is to be a redeeming community: a community where the lost can be found, the broken can be healed, and the sick can be made whole. Soon enough they see with shame the subtle, sinful barriers of race, and class, and position, and wealth that have been raised against the very house of God they love.

Who can come close to Christ without seeing his own prejudices, the cutting unkindnesses so easily perpetrated, and the sinful indifference with which one has lived? Slowly the passion grows to right those wrongs. One begins to work at rooting out the prejudices, at welcoming the drunkards and the harlots, at being as deeply and sincerely as one knows how, the redeeming community—the community that every "gathered" church, looking to Christ, must be.

Finally, as a logical consequence to the power of this spirit among the people of the gathered church, are two great works of the Spirit.

One is that such a church becomes inevitably a Spirit-filled, *believing* church. It begins, curiously, to really *believe* the great promises of the New Testament, to really believe that the Gospel is Good News to all men, and that the sick can indeed be made well, that the lame *can* walk, the blind *can* see, and the broken *can* be made whole.

It begins to see that Jesus wants us to pray not alone for the easy things, but for the hard things, the strange things, the impossible things. Briefly, it begins to become a healing church. It loses its fear of the ancient practice of the laying-on of hands. It begins to see that this is a treasure to be recovered, a ministry too long lost, a power normal and right in the Church of Christ and yet passing strange and wonderful.

No longer is a believing church ever satisfied to say to its sick: "Cheer up, time will make you well." The old clichés are traded for a new vocabulary—the vocabulary of faith, and expectancy, and power. Nothing stands in its way and its new word of faith becomes: "In the name of Jesus of Nazareth, be ye whole and well!" Before their eyes the people of a believing church soon see the miracle of the lame walking, the blind seeing, and the diseased being restored. The healing of minds, and souls, and bodies becomes part of the faith of such a church—and part of its practice. For in the heart it has begun to learn "that with God nothing shall be impossible!"

The other great work of the Spirit is that the gathered church which is honestly following Christ's leading is destined, again inevitably, to be a missionary church. You cannot love Jesus Christ and sincerely serve Him and *not* be a missionary church! Christ's whole coming was a mission. "For God so loved the world that He gave His only begotten Son, that all who believe on Him should not perish, but have everlasting life." The Master's own command was "Go ye into all the world and preach the gospel!"

It is no good *being* a church of Christ unless you believe

that out there beyond your doors is a world of a million souls perishing for want of your Gospel. It isn't just a matter of "to each his own." Christ came for all men. And He came saying: "I am the Way, the Truth and the Life." This is an imperative for the Christian Church—the imperative of a loving God who is ranging the world through us, seeking for His children. It is no arrogant, dogmatic, prideful thing, but a seeking, passionate, and winning thing.

Its range will be not only the world, with dollars and cents winging their way toward the missionary out-posts. It will be the village or city at the door-step. And it will be hours, and labor, and lives given.

And yet, the greatest mission of such a church will be the mission that runs through and through the whole of her life: the mission of the Spirit; the mission of the Spirit of Christ alive in His people and reaching out through them to wherever men are. This is the real work of the Church—being Christians wherever we go in the world! This is where the Christ in our midst would send us. For His cry is "Go ye! Go tell the people! Tell them how I died for them. Tell them how I forgive them. Tell them how I love them."

Our lives are meant to tell that love: the love that we discover through our life in the gathered church, the love that then goes out in us to tell its message to all the hearts that hunger for its truth. Surely, there can be no more exciting and exalted task in the whole world than being bearers of this Word of Life to the Children of God.

The life in the gathered church is the new life in Jesus Christ. It is the life He promised all Christians. To each it is given in his way; and ours is a great way, a way that we cherish as a precious heritage.

But this life will be nothing if it is only a heritage. The new life is to be lived. In living it there is a great and wonderful hope ahead for the churches and the people of our "Way."

6. People of the Word

In the little village where I live, in the western hills of Massachusetts, Sunday is a very special day. It is a day when, across the snow-covered fields of winter or through the heavy-leaved opulence of summer trees a bell rings, and echoes out across the valley touching the hills and ringing back, filling the morning air with music. It is a special day because, called by the bell, the people come to church. From along the hills they come and from up and down the valley road.

It is only a little church to which they come—no Gothic cathedral, no soaring monument of stone. Its timbers are the old wood of New England, and in that Puritan plain tradition it rises with those simple lines of white clapboard beauty which still speak the faith of those men who built her there. But it is a much-loved building, a building on which many hands have worked, and it is their house of God.

As the people mount the steps and take their places, they come, as Karl Barth wrote of his congregation in the Alps of Switzerland, to ask of their preacher the one great question on their hearts: "Is there any Word from the Lord?"

This is the meaning of worship—men and women coming into God's house and bowing down their lives before Him, honestly wanting to hear what He would say to them about themselves, and about life and death, and good and evil, and heaven and hell. They are people hungry for God, people eagerly devouring everything they can lay their hands on of Christian faith, people learning and preparing themselves so that one day they can go out to win men for Christ—that is what our God wants.

Because this is not only the meaning of worship; this is the meaning of the Church. Without this eagerness, without these hungry and seeking people, there is no Church! And yet these people of my village who come so gladly to their church on a Sunday morning are only a handful—a handful, compared with the hundreds who could come, a handful compared with the people—double their number —who have actually stood up in that church and accepted Christ as their Lord and covenanted to walk with Him faithfully as members one with another.

They did not mean what they said. There is no other face that can be put upon it. They have fallen away from the church because they did not mean seriously enough the promises that they made. And this is true of Congregationalism all across the country. We are one of the poorest of all denominations when it comes to worship in church.

Oh, there are many who say they are active in the church. And they are, in that old New England way. They bake lots of pies, and serve on many a supper, and pound unnumbered nails. But they are not at worship on the Sabbath day. They are not there in God's house out of love for the Lord. They are not kneeling in shame before the throne of grace, asking forgiveness. They are not pleading in the audience-chamber of the King for God's blessing and help upon their sick, and sorrowing, and sinful brethren of earth. What does it mean to be a Christian, if not this? What *could* it mean if you do not do this, at the least?

The real church is the worshipping church. This is why the extent of our failure as Congregationalists to *be* the Church is so great. Because we, of all people, are the ones who claim to be the "gathered" church, the people of the Spirit with Christ in our midst, the people who deserve to be free because Christ will lead us. We are guilty of spiritual dishonesty before God, of hypocrisy of the worst kind, to make such a claim and not to be living it.

Our uniqueness is supposed to be that we are a whole people worshipping together, working together, and led by God together: a people who bear responsibility as a whole church and not just by delegated committees or representatives. Congregationalism means literally *the congregation* —the congregation doing everything, but particularly worshipping.

As Christians of the Congregational Way, we are called to be this kind of seeking, hungering, eager "people of the Word"—people wanting above all things to hear this Word in worship. But what is there to do, seeing we have already failed so badly? Give up? The task is mountainous! Thousands of churches all across the land are in the same predicament! It seems too big even to attempt. And yet there is one thing we can do. We can care ourselves. We can learn what it means to be a Christian and a Congregationalist at worship. We can learn what our Way of worship is and then we can spread the word as the early Christians did, that it is a joyful, glorious, and blessed experience: an experience in which there is meaning, and help, and healing for every man.

The touchstone of Congregational worship is the awareness of the congregation as being a "gathered" people. This means "gathered" around Christ—not by fiat, not by authority of an ecclesiastical organization or an ecclesiastical functionary—but voluntarily, drawn only by the power of the Spirit, as long ago the disciples were drawn. It is as we become a people so gathered around Christ and His Word that our worship and all its symbols take on meaning.

The first concrete act that the New Testament shows us of such gathering around Christ was on that wonderful night of the Lord's Supper. Live it again for a moment, and see what it means for us. "Now when the even was come," says the gospel story, "He sat down with the twelve."

How simple that is, and how common to us all. ". . . when the even was come, He sat down with the twelve." This is the benediction that the evening hour brings to every man's life. This is that sacred hour when, as the great prayer says ". . . the shadows lengthen and the evening comes, and the busy world is hushed, and the fever of life is over, and our work is done," and the families of men come home at last to gather 'round a table and sit down together. All day long families are scattered and busy. But this is the one hour when they sit down to share the events of their day, to have friendship as a family, and to break together the bread which God has given; the hour which is to them so common, yet so deep, and so precious.

It was just such an hour when the tired-looking man and His twelve friends climbed up the stairs from the narrow side street in Jerusalem to a second-story room which had been prepared for supper. Darkness had already begun to fall, and it was probably by candlelight that they gathered at the table.

Still, it was different from our family gatherings. The table was not gay and laughing. For, as the shadows deepened beyond the circle of flickering light around that table, there was a kind of hush in the room as the men ate and talked quietly together. It was as if they were speaking not of the events of a day, but of the events of a lifetime. They savored of this fellowship almost as if it were to be their last supper together. There was a brooding sense that something very dear to them was ending—that something was going to happen: some strange thing that they did not understand.

Had they wandered out upon the streets that night and listened outside the Roman barracks to the cursing and the hammer blows, and seen the great cross being nailed together, they might have known. If they had even listened carefully in that upper room to the clinking of silver in the pocket of Judas, they might have known. On the face of their leader there was something they had not yet fathomed—a look of burden and sorrow, and yet a look of assurance and peace.

And then the meal was over. But, as they pushed back from the table, He whom they loved stood up and took a piece of bread, and broke it, and with that wondrous love shining in His eyes, gave it to them, saying: "Take, eat—this is my body, broken for you." And, as that piece of bread was passing from hand to hand, He took His cup and said, "All of you drink from it," for "this is my blood which is shed for you and for many, for the remission of sins. Do this, as often as you drink it, in remembrance of Me."

The sacredness of that hour and the deep meaning of that supper they scarcely realized. It was only after they had sung a hymn, and gone out into the garden, that they knew how dear it was. For it was then that the soldier's knock was heard, that the fatal kiss was given, that the cock crowed, and their Christ was killed.

Three days later, according to Luke, two of the disciples were walking to Emmaus. Rumors had been flying everywhere. A stranger joined them. "Have you heard?" they cried. "It is said that Jesus, who was crucified, is alive again!" They walked on together, talking, and at evening persuaded the stranger to stop and have supper with them at an inn. And it happened that, as they ate, the stranger took bread, and blessed it, and broke it, and gave it to them; and as the Gospel tells us, "Their eyes were opened." "Look!" they cried to one another, "The bread. The breaking of the bread. Master! Master!" And He vanished from their sight.

It was then that, with hearts beating wild with joy, they ran to tell the rest of the eleven what had happened. They too were gathered at table to eat. And even as these two from Emmaus were telling their story, it happened again. Jesus came to the table and sat down with His friends.

And we see it happening again and again as the young Church grew. In Antioch, in Corinth, in the catacombs of Rome, men and women of all kinds began looking forward to that one night of the week when they would hurry through city streets under cover of darkness, to knock softly upon the well-known door, to be welcomed into the blessed fellowship of the brethren of the Way and with them to sit once more at the simple table and partake of the sacred supper.

In any one of those secret meetings all around that Mediterranean world, it was not strange to find a common fisherman or a servant-girl drinking from the same cup and eating of the same loaf with a wealthy merchant or a veiled lady from the court of the Caesars. Because they were disciples of the Master, and were glad for the privilege of being there together at His table.

This eating and drinking together has become the great act of Christian worship. A loaf of bread, a cup of wine, and a table: so very simple and common—and yet so deep, and so meaningful. This was the wonderful experience of the early Church: a joyful experience of literally gathering around Jesus, the risen Lord. Indeed, it was so precious and sacred, that it came very soon to be observed at regular intervals as a sacrament of the Church.

But now, twenty centuries later, what do we of the Congregational Way believe about the Lord's Supper? How do we celebrate it? What are our convictions?

Look, for a moment, at what happened in history to this simple and meaningful act. It did not long remain so simple. As the centuries passed, Jesus' words, "This is my body" and "This is my blood," were distorted to mean that the bread and wine were literally and physically His body and blood, and that by repeating a formula of blessing in a process called "transubstantiation," the priest could transform a wafer and a cup of wine into the living body and blood of our Lord. The Church came to believe not that Christ's sacrifice for us had been made once and for all on Calvary, but that it was repeated again and again every time the communion was celebrated.

Gradually, the service of sharing the common cup and bread of Jesus with all the brethren, was taken away from the people. The table was pushed against the wall and called an altar. In the great cathedrals this high altar was separated from the congregation by a screen, and that room called a chancel, where only officiating priests and the monks who sang the service might enter.

After a time, this consecrated wafer, kept high on the altar as "the host," and revered as Jesus' body, was considered so sacred that often only the priest took part in the Lord's Supper.

When, in the early 16th century the Reformation came to England, it was scarcely more than King Henry's assuming for himself the authority which formerly had been the pope's. Even under Elizabeth, Anglican worship remained much the same as the Roman ritual.

Part of the struggle that produced the churches of the Congregational Way was over these rituals of the Anglican Church. The Puritans not only hated the power of the bishops, and the gaudy ritual and ornate robes of the priests at mass, but especially did they hate this separation of the communion from the people.

In their eyes, these practices were an un-Christian desecration of holy things. To those Puritan protesters, it became a matter of spiritual life and death. In Scotland the saintly Samuel Rutherford—himself a prisoner for his faith—cried out in Puritan outrage: "And what shall be the day of the silent and dumb watchman of Scotland? Where will we leave our glory and what if Christ depart out of our land?"

This was the spirit of those who protested what they called Elizabeth's "Black Rubric" of kneeling at communion. Many came to New England, as did one of my family ancestors, Gregory Stone, for the very reason that he refused to "kneel to any priest" to receive communion.

The communion practice of the Congregational Way,

which we share with the whole Protestant Reformed tradition, was, as in so much else that they did, an attempt to get back to the purity of the original New Testament practice.

To them, the Lord's Supper was what they called a "Gospel" sacrament. This is not only because it was instituted and practiced in the gospels, but because this very act itself is a proclamation of the Gospel. This is why our fathers insisted that the preaching of the Word must always accompany the celebration of the Lord's Supper. For the Lord's Supper is an *acting* of the Gospel message, just as preaching is the *speaking* of that message.

When the Son of God stood up in that dimly lit room ages ago and cried: "This bread is my body broken for you, and this cup is my blood poured out for you," He was proclaiming the whole message of God to man. He did that night with bread and wine the very thing that, in the providence of God, He would do next day upon the cross. His body *was* broken for us. His blood *was* poured out for us. In Jesus Christ, God did this great thing for us.

There are some Congregationalists who say that communion is only a remembrance, a commemoration. I would die if that were all that it was! No; when Jesus said the bread and wine were His body and blood, I believe He was promising that whenever we share in His Supper as a sacrament, He would come and be with us just as surely as He was there with the twelve in the Upper Room. In this service then, Christ is here, not in the flesh and not just in memory; but really, truly, and actually present among His people in the power of His Spirit. He is here as a Person— the Son of the Living God—welcoming us, and bidding us to sit down with Him to receive the Bread of Life.

The Congregational view of communion was, first, that it is a "Gospel" sacrament. Their second belief was that in it Christ is "really" present—not physically nor just as a memory. Their third conviction was that the Lord's table is a free table, and that all who love Him are welcome to sit down with Him.

The forgiveness and new life He gives is free. Freely, as an act of love, Christ died for *all* men. So also, then, is the bread and wine of the Lord's Supper a free gift, given in the open fellowship of the table of the whole family of believers. Who are we to say who shall come and who shall not? Has any man the right to say that only those confirmed in the Roman, or the Episcopal, or the Baptist Church may eat at Christ's table? The Master knows whom He has invited. "I come not to condemn the world, but that the world, through me, might be saved!" The *world*—Christ died for all men. So if the Lord's Supper really does "show the Lord's death till He come," it must be given to all men who love Him and intend to serve Him. The Lord's table is, with us, a free table, and our communion is "open" communion.

And finally, there was another concern our fathers had for communion which goes straight to the heart of all their symbolism of the Lord's Supper. The story says that "when the even was come, He *sat down* with the twelve." He made Himself equal, He became one of them, He created a fellowship.

Therefore, in the classical Reformed and Congregational view, an altar set high against a wall in a chancel where only the priest can come is wrong. In our tradition it is always "the table"—never "the altar!" We find in the New Testament no grounds for an altar. It was a table at which

Jesus, and Peter, and Andrew, and Matthew, and Judas and the others ate their last meal together. They sat *around* it —a fellowship of friends, a family of God. Jesus did not stand in front of it changing robes, ringing bells, swinging incense, with the disciples barred from the sacred supper by a wooden railing! It was a meal—not a sacrifice: a common meal of bread and wine made sacred by the redeeming presence of the Living Christ. So our communion is at a table, not an altar.

The great symbol of Congregationalism then, is the Table. In the earliest Protestant churches, long wooden tables were often put right down the center aisle of the church, so that all the congregation could actually sit around them. But today, where that is not possible, the table is kept out in the open where the congregation can at least be symbolically seated around it.

I believe it is when you and I come so close to the Lord, as His own Table, that His purity and love show us up in all our unworthiness. This is when we are moved to repentance and confession. This is when we are made ready to receive the unspeakable gift of His forgiving love in the broken bread and the poured out wine.

Never shall I forget a communion service I once attended in one of the little store-front churches of the East Harlem Protestant Parish in New York City. It was Maundy Thursday evening. We had to walk down a narrow, dark, rickety stairway. In a poorly lighted and low-ceilinged room two long rough tables were set for a meal. They were placed in the form of a cross. No one spoke as the people filed in —some old folks, some children, several whole families. They were of all sorts—Italian, Negro and Puerto Rican. A young minister came in and the service began. But as he said the words of Jesus, he broke a great loaf of bread, and that loaf itself went from hand to hand—each one breaking off a piece. And as the loaf went around that table, I suddenly realized that all these people were softly singing. It was the words of the spiritual—"Let us break bread together on our knees."

The same thing happened with the wine—"Let us drink wine together on our knees . . ." No one laughed or was embarrassed. Here, amongst all that humble congregation, something real and powerful was happening. They were living again the Last Supper. For those people, with all their different languages and colors, and for me, the simple table of the Master had taught the great truth of the Christian faith. We went from that room and that rude table as newborn disciples of the Risen Christ. Not one of us walked into that Maundy Thursday night who did not know in his heart that the Lord was with him.

Whether in Congregationalism or any other Church Way, this is what the Lord's Supper was meant to do. We believe it happens most truly when, as long ago, Christians sit down together at His Table.

But in Congregationalism it is not only the Table which holds the center of the people's attention. There is also the pulpit and the open Bible upon it. For the other great "Gospel Sacrament" of our Way is the preaching of the Word of God.

One of the features of worship in the medieval Roman Church which most disturbed the Reformers was the lack

as he said the words of Jesus, he broke a great loaf of

was. God had a Word, they believed, to speak to His people. And this Word could be known in the Bible. In this Book was the Word of life and truth that God had spoken through inspired men for all time. It was the one great authority for Christian people, and beside it the pope and all the decrees of Rome were nothing. And only out of this Book could God's Word be read and proclaimed. So the pulpit and its open Bible became another central symbol in early Reformation worship and in the Congregational worship which followed.

In a time when the Bible had been for a thousand years the sole possession of the clergy, those courageous reformers jeopardized their lives by storming that medieval sanctuary of exclusiveness to bring this Word of God back to the common people.

For the vast majority of ordinary folk in sixteenth-century Germany, the Bible had been a strange, mysterious, and almost unknown book. Chained to the pulpit of the priests and read to the people in an ancient tongue, it was kept so far from them that they had hardly an inkling of what it was about, and certainly no notion of the life-giving power that was locked within its pages.

And then a monk named Brother Martin—later known to the world as Martin Luther—translated that Book of books from its distant Latin into the common German of the people. The printing press produced scores of copies, and almost overnight hundreds of peasant homes were hearing for the first time the forbidden but wonderful Word of God.

Farmers, laborers, and tradesmen began to read how God had entered human life in Christ Jesus and had confronted other simple men like themselves with His amazing love.

They read that Bible message until it sang like good news in their hearts and the fires of faith began to glow anew.

What the reformers and their people found in the Bible was not an ancient manuscript preserved for centuries. They did not find in it a valuable source book of archaeology, with myths and legends to be unraveled and examined by critical scholarship. It was not even for them a collection of the most beautiful and inspired writing of all literature. Wonderful as all these things might be, they were nothing to what those men actually did find. For them, this Book was the Word of God.

For those first Protestants the Bible was a living thing. When they opened its covers the heavens opened too, and God spoke. Under its spell they stood out on the horizons of eternity and saw the first dawn rise, and heard the morning stars sing together on the day of creation.

They felt the earth shake and the thunder roll on Sinai's height when God chose Israel for His people and gave His Word in stone; they heard the angel chorus shatter the still air with singing on the night when the child was born; and they saw the love of God nailed to a cross on that dark day when the Lord Christ died. They were there, and whenever God confronted the men of the Bible, He confronted them.

But even more than this, they saw power in the Bible: power to set multitudes of common people free from superstition and fear; power to reform and heal a sick Church; power to deal decisively with all the complex enigmas of their sixteenth-century life. For them, the Bible was nothing less than Jesus Christ Himself striding through their lives with all the power of God.

No wonder Luther, Calvin, Knox, and the others could

say, "This Book is the Word of God. It has spoken to us." They reverenced it so much that the very opening of the Bible in public worship became—like the breaking of bread —a sacramental act. Those thrilling words: "Hear the Word of God," meant to those hushed congregations that God was about to speak to His people.

This Bible which these men rediscovered became the armor and glory of life for themselves and for all the Christian generations to follow. It was only right then, that behind and above the Table of the Lord should stand open on the pulpit this wonderful Book of the Lord. The whole of reformation worship—its structure and its words—was built upon this Book.

The Bible was there in the center of the congregation to read from, of course. But that was not enough. If men and women were to understand what the Bible was saying, it must be expounded, explained, and proclaimed through the voice of men. And this act of proclaiming the Bible's message, of telling among men the glorious good news of Christ which the apostles had told before them, was called preaching—the preaching of the Word of God.

It was this act of telling the "old, old story" through the voice and personality of a man on fire with its joy, that became the great and peculiar act of Protestant worship. This was the climax of the service, the message that the people came to hear, and all that went before—the singing of the hymns, the bowing in prayer, the reading of the Scriptures—were meant to lead the people up the slopes of breathless expectancy to this greatest moment of their praise and worship.

I do not mean that all that went before was mere preliminary. Such an idea has always been false and perverse in Protestant thinking. Every part of it, from call to worship through Scripture and prayers were meant to lead men's hearts from the threshold of worship deeper and deeper toward the great holy of holies of proclamation. They were to open their hearts, and thrill their minds, and prepare their spirits to receive the Word that God would speak that day.

So it was that the churches of the Reformation became known as "preaching" churches. And in this tradition the churches of the Congregational Way fully share. If Christ was really in the midst of His gathered people, how else could He speak to them if not through preaching? This, according to the Congregational fathers, was the greatest way in worship through which their Lord would come. Preaching, therefore, was always central—central in their thinking, and central physically in the place of the pulpit and Bible in the midst of the people. The people, to their mind, must literally be gathered *around* the Word—around the pulpit, around the Bible, and around the preacher. They were a people of the Word.

And yet, they never let go their controlling belief that Christ was among them in His Spirit, that He was there Himself—free and strong, knowing the hearts of men and moving always as He willed to those who needed Him the most. Never did they think for a moment that they had Christ captured in the Bible, that they could chain Him to set forms or words. His was a free Spirit, and our seventeenth-century forebears believed with all their hearts that their worship of Him must be "free" worship.

These were not men who took lightly the great tradition of the Church. They did not scoff at the prayers of beauty which belonged to the ages—the words of devotion with which an Augustine, or a Savonarola, or a Bernard, or an Aquinas had come to God. The great prayers of the Church and the great traditions they were glad to keep. Their concern was to purify, to reach back if they could to New Testament practice.

They looked for balance. For, while the prayers of the ages were beautiful and strong, they sensed a freedom and a freshness sweeping through the worship of the Apostolic Church. They saw Paul, led by the Spirit to proclaim His word in Athens, trusting often that God himself would give him words to say. They saw them all—young Timothy and Barnabas, Paul and Peter—moved by the Spirit and folding their hands to pray.

Those early Congregationalists wanted to be open to worship like that. They wanted to be free. They wanted to be expectant. They wanted their Christ to come among them and do *His* will, not theirs. And so Congregational worship has always been "free worship." We stand for freedom in preaching and freedom in prayer. The Church year is there for a preacher to follow, but it is there as a help and never a law. Only God knows what His people must hear on a given Sabbath day in one city here, or another one there. And only a preacher with his heart open and his Bible before him will know that Word and be able to speak it. We expect this openness in our ministers' preaching: an openness to the special Word of the time of crisis, and an openness too, to the pattern and swell of the Christian year, from Advent to Christmas, and through Lent to Easter, that the whole counsel of God may be heard by His "people of the Word."

We expect the same openness in our preacher's prayers. We are grateful to know, when he leads us in prayer, that it is *his* heart's words that gather us up, *his* spirit that swells and leads and draws us on until together we stand at the mercy seat in the very presence of God, to be judged and healed. We want no borrowings at this intimate time—no beautiful words from another age—but only the stumbling, humbling words of the shepherd-heart who, along with God, loves us as his flock. The leading of the Spirit in preaching and in prayer is the essence of "free worship" for us.

It is in the free worship of this "gathered community" that one important symbol remains to be mentioned. It is so obvious and yet so subtle that it is rarely even thought of as a symbol. In this whole life of preaching the Word at the pulpit, and acting the Word at the Table, *the people* themselves are a symbol!

As they gather in quiet wonder and expectancy at the hour of worship waiting for the Bread of Life to be broken to them, either at the pulpit or at the Table, the people symbolize the very essence of worship in our Congregational Way. They are the congregation, and—with the exception of Christ Himself—they are everything to us.

The very standard under which we rally as Congregationalists, is the word of Jesus to which we turn again and again: "Where two or three are gathered together in My Name, *there* am I in the midst of them." We believe that Jesus called His disciples to be a People: that it was when they *gathered together*, believing, that he would come to them. The pitiful picture of a Roman mass or an Anglican evensong being sung in an empty cathedral with priests, choir boys, but no congregation—despite the beauty of the sanctuary—just has no meaning in the Congregational Way. It is not worship at all! A beautiful tableau, perhaps, but not worship. Christ meant worship to be of the *people*.

Not that He asks for a multitude. Two or three are enough. But there must be two or three. For it is to them that He promised to come.

When the people do gather together around the Table and around the pulpit they are symbolizing physically their life as a fellowship. They are telling the world, "We belong together. We are a brotherhood—a sharing, praying, working, believing band of brothers, bound together by our Lord Christ!"

Such a gathered people are living testimony to the sense of community in Christ, of "koinonia" as the Greek has it, which from the very earliest days has been the essence of the Christian life. The whole power of the early Church was in the fact that it was a fellowship, a family of God who deeply loved and cared for one another because they loved Christ. This was their power! In a service of the Lord's Supper, for instance, the whole loaf of bread itself indicates again that we are one body, a family of caring in the household of God. Indeed, as the Congregational Union of England and Wales says about communion: "The true celebrants are the whole company, for whom the deacons and minister are no more than the appointed agents— themselves but fellow-guests and fellow-members of the household of faith."

Because of this conviction that the Christian community is a fellowship, we see the gathering of Christian people at the Lord's Table as a corporate act—as something we do together. This is why the very architecture of most of our sanctuaries insists that the communion table be not away from the people in a recessed chancel, but out in the sanctuary in the midst of the people just as any family supper-table would be, with the pews symbolically grouped around it. This is also why we do not come forward individually to a communion rail, but pass the bread and wine so that the whole congregation can eat and drink together. This is why, in my little church, at the end of every communion service we symbolically clasp hands down each row singing, "Blest be the tie that binds." Even when we take communion to shut-ins it is never thought of as private communion but as the Lord's Supper being brought from the table of the fellowship to the dear ones who, through prayer and love, though not through physical presence, are still a part of that fellowship.

This sense of the People as a symbol runs even through such ordinary acts as congregational singing and congregational praying. Christianity has always been a singing faith and our singing together today can be a sign of our oneness as a people in Christ. Surely, the great singing in Congregational churches should be the singing of the people, and not the paid perfection of the professional soloists, quartets, and even choirs which haunt so many of our churches. How can professionals, who are not in any sense a part of the gathered community and sometimes not even believers, possibly compare with the joyous song of a whole congregation singing "When I Survey the Wondrous Cross," or "Jesus Shall Reign Where'er the Sun!" If anything, we must have less of professional choirs, and more of volunteer choirs dedicated primarily to leading the people in the singing of hymns.

As with music, so also with prayer. We do wrong to think that only the minister prays in public worship. Prayers that the people say aloud together are all to the good, but even when they are not praying aloud, even when in the pastoral prayer the words are the pastor's, how can we say the people are not praying? We need to understand the pastoral prayer more and more for what it is—the gathering up of the prayers of the whole people together in one voice, and yet being prayed with silent power by every person in that congregation. Any preacher knows that one of the most moving moments in the whole service is that time of prayer in which he finds himself held up and strengthened on all sides by the silent but real prayers of a loving people.

The people themselves, then, are one of the great symbols of our Congregational worship. It is so because we are a fellowship of Christians, a band of brothers, whom Christ Himself has gathered together.

Now Protestantism in America has been living recently through a series of decades in which all of us, at least in liberal circles, have been saying that we were essentially the same. "One church is just the same as another," was the cry, "no differences here!" And thank God for the spirit of openness, and tolerance, and understanding with which we have been able to meet across denominational lines and honestly recognize that we do love the same Lord. And yet, in the process, we have forgotten what was uniquely our own, what was our peculiar witness to make in the life of Christ's whole Church.

The truth is that we do have a witness to make, a great doctrine of the church to proclaim, a precious heritage to understand and to share with our fellow-Christians. And the very heart of it is our concept of the gathered church and of our life in worship as a people of the Word. For me there is something wonderfully exciting here which has an important word to say, not only about the meaning of our worship itself, but also—and quite logically—about the kind of building in which our worship should take place. Therefore, I propose to add to this chapter on Congregational worship a "concluding unscientific postscript" about Congregational architecture.

Churches all over America are building these days: building new additions, building new churches, building whole new plants. Church architecture is commanding more and more attention, with two or three professional magazines dedicated exclusively to its study and promotion, and other theological and church journals of long standing giving it increased space and prominence.

As with all other building today, the great interest is in modern functional design. Everywhere one reads the praises sung of almost any new church which ventures into some striking modern pattern of design. The hue and cry from nearly all quarters is to forsake the traditional, to get away from the meaningless forms of the past, and to create in brick and stone some symbol of what our own time, our own generation is saying. "Express the faith of today—not the outworn faith of yesterday!" they say.

Church leaders and theologians alike seem bent on wooing the artists, on bridging the gulf between the Church and the arts—a completely worthy aim. Of course the Church wants to influence culture, to communicate and converse with the poets and dramatists, the novelists and the artists! Would that we might *have* a few Michelangelos and Raphaels in the Church of today!

But we do not. Not yet, at least. And yet, curiously, even the theologians themselves seem to have completely turned over to the artists and architects the task of thinking out and conceiving the new forms of the Church. They are allowing the criteria for church architecture to be art and not theology.

It is some of these very theologians who cry aloud that the faith of today is shallow and inadequate. Why, then, should we be so quick to express this faith of today in our new architecture? Is the traditional, the past, so terrible? Perhaps the Christian gospel which is the same yesterday, today, and forever has something to say to our time and our generation. Perhaps it has a Word to speak to us which we are reluctant to hear. Perhaps it is this Word which ought to be speaking to the world through the architecture of our churches. It is not the spirit of our time, the neuroses of our generation which should shine through our church buildings, but the eternal Word of God!

The sad story of so many new church buildings and sanctuary remodelings in Congregationalism today is the effort to achieve something that is "nice"—something "aesthetic," something "tasteful." Some of the poorest, vaguest writing about what a church sanctuary should look like is being written today in the magazines of church architecture and furnishing. They talk of "atmosphere" and "spirit" with the same pale religiosity which afflicts so many modern Christians. Indeed, they express what too many church members feel.

Congregationalists, at least, by the score, are—in the name of "progress"—throwing out the old center pulpits from their churches and building in divided chancels where structurally, they were never meant to be. In fairness, it should be said that many of them are concerned to bring back some of the forms of beauty which our Puritan forebears too quickly discarded. We allow organs now, why not a cross and perhaps even candles? But by-and-large the standard for the radical return to chancels and altars is that they are "nice." What a lovely setting for the bride and groom at weddings! What a dignified atmosphere and increased formality when the minister can walk about the chancel, reading the Bible from one side and preaching from the other. How fine to have a cross and attractive flower arrangements to center our attention, rather than the minister and his bare pulpit and Bible!

What we do not understand when we do these things to our churches is that we are going back to the very concept of religion against which the reformers rebelled. We are again taking the Lord's Table away from the people, putting it in another room in which the people do not even sit, and calling it an altar. With the minister no longer standing behind the Table at communion as Jesus did, we are changing the very nature of the sacrament from supper to sacrifice. We are tearing aside the great traditions of pulpit and Bible, and saying what many modern churchmen believe, that preaching is secondary—the liturgy first. So many forget that without preaching we die, and for lack of great preaching many congregations are already dying.

Yet all we have been saying in this chapter on worship has implications for architecture. The "people of the Word," gathered around Christ, sitting about His Table, hearing His Word, being a fellowship—these very ideas suggest a shape and form which could speak to our time and especially to us Congregationalists about how our church building should be built.

The early churches of the Reformation have already

set the basic lines we can follow. In an oblong sanctuary the pulpit was often against the wall on one of the long sides with the Table before it and the congregation grouped *around* them on all three sides. Protestant churches, and particularly Congregational churches, need not be auditoriums at all with the people stretching away in rows down a long, narrow nave. One of the most significant modern churches today is a Presbyterian church in the West where the congregation forms a kind of horseshoe curve around a dominating long center table, with the pulpit at the open end of the horseshoe form. The general plan of this church represents an exciting new attempt to say something with rare theological integrity through the architectural forms of today. This is a direction which all of us could take.

Why not have a table at which the people can literally be seated? And why not a pulpit and a Word around which they may also sit? And why not be so curved that the family of God can, in a sense, face each other and know themselves as a fellowship in Christ? In the Presbyterian church just mentioned, no person can sit more than twenty feet from the table.

For those of us who are probably destined—happily, I think—to worship in the traditional meeting houses of Puritan New England, there is surely some hope. We may never be the builders of a new church with the opportunity to use all the new materials and designs we would like. But perhaps our task is to look long and hard at what we already have, and fill with meaning what may have become assumed and ordinary.

Those who decry the white spires of New England and the old churches beneath them make a great mistake. It is not my experience that these buildings have lost meaning for their people. For many folk of New England towns, this *is* the church. It has been there for centuries. They have labored on it and loved it. The faith of generations has hallowed it. In their simple way, this place that they know is their Holy of holies.

It is not just a monument. They *are* keeping up with the times. They are heating it, preserving it, modernizing and adding to it—often with the best of advice and most modern means. We should not be too quick to discard these buildings of beauty. They represent a grace and craft we cannot create nor afford with the materials and the craftsmen of today. There is something good in these buildings and in the regard of their people for them. There is care, there is love. Offending all this is no virtue in itself.

The danger so obvious is to live in the past: to let the forms of the past chain us to a faith of the past until we have no understanding and no word we can say to today.

Our task is to charge the old forms with the meaning eternal which our fathers were saying in their way to their time. It is to teach the people of our Way, the gathered people, the people of the Word who they are and what their witness is. For many of us the pulpit is still there, and the table too, in the midst of the people where they belong.

What our people do not know is *why* they are there, and how God can use these symbols and forms. And what they need to know too, is how God could use *them*. How mighty they could be if one day they might see that they have a wonderful destiny—a destiny to be, as they gather each week, a people of the Word, coming together in faith and then going out with that Word in their hearts to tell it to the world.

7. "Raised Up to Minister"

One of the truest and most terrifying sentences in the Old Testament is the one which testifies: "It is a fearful thing to fall into the hands of the Living God!" No man knows this fear more surely than the Christian minister. For, from the days of a Moses trembling before a hillside bush aflame with the glory of God, down to our own day, the men whom God has called to serve Him have quaked before His voice and feared to answer Him. Moses himself knew a hundred reasons why he was not the man to go to Pharoah. Jonah took ship to Tarshish to flee the bidding voice of God. And Jeremiah the prophet protested: "Ah, Lord God! Behold I cannot speak; for I am a child." Even Peter, on that day at the lakeside before the Lord, hid his face and cried out: "Depart from me Lord, for I am a sinful man!" And who of us does not know in his heart this terrible impossibility of being what God calls him to be, because he is a sinful man.

I know now what was meant when one of the greatest ministers in my life, my father, said: "Stay away from the ministry until you just can't help yourself." The tasks before a man in the ministry are mountainous: a whole lifetime spent on the edge of human despair, striving with such poor talents to preach the Gospel to the poor, to heal the broken-hearted, to deliver the captives, to give sight to the blind, and to set at liberty them that are bruised!

Richard Baxter, that great Puritan Divine of the English church once said that preaching was speaking "as a dying man to dying men," and so it is. The most glorious good news that ever the ears of man did hear, the message they must hear or perish, and you so poor a vessel to proclaim it! A man must love God and love men with everything he has, or it is no good even trying to be a minister.

And yet men do become ministers. They enter its life gladly, with hearts singing in spite of their fears, giving up careers in any number of other fields to live this life of poor reward and impossible achievement at the call of the wandering carpenter who says only "Come," and they come.

What does it mean then, in our Congregational Way, to be a minister? What is our understanding of the ministry? What is its role in the life of the gathered people? Has it anything unique about it? Is it any different in our Way than it is in other traditions? These are the questions for which we will seek answers in this chapter on those among us who are "raised up to minister."

The first concern is how one comes to *be* a minister in the Congregational Way. Ministers do not materialize out of the thin air, nor have they been all their lives standing in those pulpits where now we know them. Somewhere they were nurtured and prepared. Somewhere they met the Master and heard His call. Somewhere they bent their minds and hearts in prayer and study. And somewhere they were first made one with a people of God and learned at their hands the meaning of preaching and of being a pastor to the needs of men.

Where is it then, from whence such a man comes? He comes from *out of the life of a gathered church.* From the very beginning of the Congregational Way this was one of its great ideas: that the minister of a Congregational church is "raised up" from among the people; raised up *from* the people to minister *to* the people. A man was actually ordained to the ministry of a particular church, with at least the theoretical assumption that he would serve that church for life, and with the very definite assumption that he would be found from within the Congregational fellowship and with a minimum of "stealing" from sister churches.

In Northampton, just down the road from my village, the famed Jonathan Edwards came to the pulpit of the old First Church in very much this way. After growing up in East Windsor, Connecticut, he came to the church in Northampton which his grandfather Stoddard had been serving for years, became his grandfather's assistant, and very soon began his own famous pastorate there. In early New England, because ministers were settled in their first church, often for life, this kind of thing was more easily possible than it is today.

But the idea proclaims two great truths. One is that the minister is one of the people: he is a man as they are men and as Jesus was a man; he knows their humanity and shares it with them. The other is that the Church itself—every local, gathered church of Christ—bears direct responsibility for nurturing, for training, for "raising up" its own ministry.

How many churches of the Congregational Way today see this as their responsibility—indeed, as their exciting privilege? How many ministers for the whole of Christ's Church have been raised up during the last fifty years in your church or in mine? We ought to ask ourselves this question.

In a Roman Catholic family today, the most wonderful thing that could possibly happen to one of the sons—and indeed, to the whole family through him—is for that young man to become a priest. What a wonderful, glowing pride lights the eyes of many an old Irish mother when she tells about her son who is a priest. Can we match that? Can most families in our Congregational churches even touch that? "No son of mine is going to be a minister!" is a comment that has been heard in my parish and in many another like it. "What kind of a life is that," some say, "with every one talking about you, and not paying you enough to live on?"

Hardly the sort of talk that is likely to enthuse our young men to consider the ministry! We *do* talk about our ministers—and not always kindly. It is so easy to criticize, to forget the devotion, and the study, and the years that have gone into his training, and not to see the ways he may be trying and the good he may be doing. How different if we sensed an excitement about this calling: if we saw in it what Dr. Raymond Calkins called "the romance of the ministry!" How different if we followed our minister out on his pastoral rounds each day with our prayers, or if we held him up in those same prayers during the hours of the morning when he is toiling over his sermon. To love, and respect, and bear with the man whom God in His wisdom has sent to be our pastor would make such a difference in encouraging and thrilling our own sons and the young men of our churches with the calling of the ministry.

As a people we have a great obligation. Several hundred Congregational churches in America are without pastors.

Where will they come from? They must come from the churches. These young men must come from churches where sincerely committed lay Christians come to know them, and care about them, and become their friends, and talk with them, and pray for them, and one day present to them the claims of Christ upon their lives for the ministry.

But a man comes to be a minister also *from being called by God*. The seed can be sown by loving friends and by Christian families. It can be nurtured by the gathered church through the years of growth. But no man can be claimed for the ministry until he has been called by God.

I remember the protest so often made by Dr. Billy Graham when people told him what a great preacher he was: "If God should once take his hands off my life, these lips would turn to clay and this voice would cease to speak." He knew what every great minister of the Gospel knows, that without God's call, and without God's work to do, and without God's hand upon him, his ministry would be utterly without power.

Men are called to the Christian ministry just as Andrew, and Peter, and Matthew were called. They are called when Christ the Lord stands across their path and says "Come, follow Me." It may not be as it was with an Isaiah, who, standing one day in the flickering candlelight of the temple, saw the Lord high and lifted up and calling "Whom shall I send, and who will go for us?" It may be nothing as cataclysmic as that. It may rather be something as simple as the sight of a hungry child in a ruined country. It may be the growing sense of a world's aching need realized in the years of youth, or it may be simply the word of a friend when the heart is right. God works in strange and wondrous ways and His means of reaching young men for the ministry is infinite and varied.

The great thing is that the call *comes* and that he who would minister never forgets that it *did* come, and that He who called is beside him still.

There is yet another way too, that a man comes to be a minister in the churches of our Way: He is *educated*. This is not always true in every denomination. In some churches the call is enough. Not so in the Congregational Way. The call is important—yea, it is the very touch of the divine upon any man's work. But education is needed.

Even Jesus and Paul never ministered without learning. The forty days in the wilderness as well as the preparation of his youth were certainly such days for the master, and Paul we are told went from Damascus to the desert to learn of his Christ, to grow in the message before he told it to men.

One of the proudest traditions of the Congregational Way in America is its tradition of an educated ministry. Let a man be nurtured in the Church, by all means, and let him hear the call of God. But let him not be sent among the people without the wisdom and the grace of learning. The very presence of the Harvards, and the Yales, and the Amhersts among us is because our forebears insisted that there should never cease to be for the churches "an educated ministry."

There was a time in early New England when the minister was often the only educated person in the community. He it was who had read, and traveled, and studied, and learned. This is no longer true. And yet how much more important now, with college graduates, and a host of intelligent, well-read folk in our congregations, that our ministers be educated, and *well*-educated.

There is so much more one needs to know to be an intelligent man today: literature and art, world affairs and science, humanities and history. The mind can scarcely encompass the knowledge of today. By comparison, it seems little enough that ministers of Christ have four years of hard study in the liberal arts and sciences before attempting their three years of seminary. Even then the Bible, theology, psychology, and Church history are themselves such mere beginnings in a minister's understanding.

For education is more: It is people, it is places; it is good books and far travels; it is knowing oneself, it is knowing the world. The ministry is a high calling, and, in our Way, it demands a high standard. One of the best ways of keeping that standard high is the demand for education.

And here again, we Congregational people would do well to accept our obligation. Education is expensive—expensive for students, expensive for institutions. How better could our prospering churches be spending their money than on seminaries and men? If we raise up the men, we must give them the best.

Finally, one comes to be a minister *by being called to a church and by being ordained.* Ordination and the call to a church I mention together advisedly. For in many Protestant traditions a man is ordained to the Christian ministry in general. In a sense, he is ordained into the ministry of the whole Church of Christ.

But the Congregational understanding of ordination is different. Our whole understanding of the Church is that it is made visible concretely and physically in the life of local gathered churches. Some of us would say that it is *only* here in a local church that the life of the whole Church of Christ is made visible. The Church, our Congregational fathers believed, had its truest life in those places where its people were actually gathered together face-to-face as Christian friends around Jesus Christ in a continuing community relationship. They believed in the *invisible* church, of course—the Church militant and triumphant, made up of that great cloud of witnesses in heaven and on earth who are the church past, present, and future. But they insisted that the visible Church was most truly the Church wherever it was a local gathered company of believers with Christ in their midst. The Savoy Declaration leaves no question on this score when it states in Article VI of the Polity section: "Besides these particular Churches, there is not instituted by Christ any Church more extensive or Catholique entrusted with power for the administration of his ordinances, or the execution of any authority in His name."

This understanding of the Church inevitably determined their understanding of ordination. If the Church's life was manifested in local gathered churches, then—as far as the early Congregational fathers were concerned—a candidate for the ministry should be ordained only to the ministry of such a local gathered church. Ministers in early New England were considered to be ordained to minister to the church they had been called to serve, and if they left that church they ceased to be ministers until called and ordained to the ministry of another church.

Such a doctrine of the Church has interesting implications. One is the question of who has the right to ordain in Congregationalism. Today it is customary for a church wanting its pastor ordained to call an ecclesiastical council of neighboring churches to come and examine their minister as to faith and calling, and then to proceed "with the church" to ordain him. It is easy for Congregational Associations, misunderstanding their authority, to think that they are the bodies with the sole right to ordain or to withhold ordination.

Actually, it is the church itself in which Christ has vested this authority. In calling an ecclesiastical council a Congregational church is extending to its sister churches a privilege of fellowship. It is inviting them to *share* with it in the ordination as friends, but not as an authoritative body. The Savoy Declaration makes it quite clear that "The Eldership of the Church"—in other words, the Deacons of a church today—are the actual people through whom a gathered church ordains its pastor. In Article XI of the section on polity it affirms that

> "The way appointed by Christ for the calling of any person, fitted and gifted by the Holy Ghost, unto the office of Pastor, Teacher, or Elder in a Church, is, that he be chosen thereunto by the common suffrage of the Church itself, and solemnly set apart by Fasting and Prayer, *with Imposition of hands of the Eldership of that Church* . . ." (Italics mine).

The idea of ordination in the abstract to the ministry of the whole Church simply by a group of other already-ordained ministers is specifically ruled out, when Savoy, in Article XV says

> "Ordination alone without the Election or precedent consent of the Church, by those who formerly have been ordained by virtue of that Power they have received by their Ordination, doth not constitute any person a Church-Officer, or communicate Office-power to him."

156

This is why even today no young man may be ordained to the Congregational ministry until he has first received a call from a particular church. People of the Congregational Way wishing to live out the full implications of their tradition might well consider doing what some of our churches are already doing, study the possibility of having the Deacons of a church perform the laying-on-of-hands at Ordination as a testimony to the church's primary role.

The other question raised by our view of the Church and its Ordination is that of who, in our fellowship, is to be called a minister. Certainly our 17th-century fathers believed a minister to be raised up to serve the people of God in a local church—to proclaim to them regularly the Word of God, to administer to them the sacraments, to be their faithful and loving pastor going in and out among them and sharing with them all the burdens and joys of life in the name of Christ. The act of ministering our Congregational fathers saw as something most concrete and continuing, and as having to do with people.

What does this say of those necessary and important people who today serve among us as theological teachers and as denominational executives? They have all been ordained to the Christian ministry and some of them once served particular churches. Probably because the nature of the Church's life has changed over the years to necessitate central offices and their staffs no one would feel that they should be denied ordination when they go from their parishes to serve a denominational agency or to teach in a seminary.

But should they be called ministers? The teachers have perhaps the best claim. Early Congregational churches often had both an ordained Teacher and an ordained Minister.

And yet there *is* a difference. A man teaching in a seminary or serving a board is *not* ministering. He is not regularly preaching the Word to the same people, administering the sacraments to them, or being their pastor.

A theological teacher usually does not even call himself a minister. He thinks of himself as being called by God to be a teacher, and his work as teaching. It is much harder for the denominational executive who may once have been a minister but is no longer. Perhaps a small testimony all of us could make to the vitality of the Congregational doctrine of the Church and the Ministry is to be quite honest in designating those who serve God among us in different ways. Let him who is a Director or a Secretary be *called* a Director or Secretary; let him who is a Teacher be called a Teacher; and let him who is a Minister be called a Minister!

These then, are the steps by which a man comes to the ministry in the Congregational Way. He comes from the life of a gathered church, he is called by God, he is educated, and he is called to serve a particular church and is ordained.

But there is another sense in which the question of who is a minister in Congregationalism must be considered. The idea that a minister is "raised up" from among the people to serve as their pastor and preacher is testimony to our conviction that he is not only one of the people but that *all of the people are ministers*. Congregationalism takes with complete seriousness Luther's doctrine of the "priesthood of all believers."

In the area of ministry the emphasis of our Way is again upon the congregation, upon the responsibility of each member of the church to be a minister: to love the brethren, to heal the sick, to feed the hungry, to clothe the poor, to comfort the sorrowing, and to watch with the dying. This is what it means to *be* a Congregation: to have real pastoral duties, real concern for the needs of people, and sincere willingness to give oneself in serving those needs.

And yet, how tragically we fail to live this obligation of the Congregational Way. We were all meant to be pastors, and our deacons to be "under-shepherds" with the minister, yet most Congregational people do not seem to realize that this is part of their duty and privilege as Congregational Christians. There is the idea among us that this is a professional job, something lay people are not to be bothered with: "Let the minister do it—that's what he is paid for!"

Of course the minister will do it as far as the time and energies of one dedicated man will allow. But the fact is that in no church, no matter how efficient and well organized, are all the pastoral needs of the people met, or even known. It is sheer physical impossibility. Yet, how often there are lay people, neighbors and friends, who *do* know the needs, who see the crises of life develop, and who could go into those homes and minister with power if only they realized that this is their mission and their calling. The problem is primarily that lay people feel themselves not competent, not equal to the grief and trouble they will find. This, surely, should be one of the great areas of teaching in our Congregational Way, for the competence that is needed is power in prayer, love of God, love of people, and the shepherd-heart.

This view of church membership and service is completely in keeping with our view of the ministry. For the minister among us is not of a higher order, but a different one. It is almost a matter of time. The minister is called and set apart to do full-time what all the rest of the congregation are trying to do part-time. Not all can be ministers in the fullest sense. Not all have the ability, not all have the call, and certainly not all have the time. Some must be carpenters, some must be housewives, some must be bankers, some must be teachers. And all can be ministers where they live. The Church's greatest work is to be done by these lay people in the world—at the shop, in the home, on the street. Our ministry as lay people is to the world, to our fellow human beings in their crying need for God and His salvation.

But some man must be their guide; some man must be their teacher; some man must give his life to searching the treasures of the Bible and proclaiming them to the people; some man must be a minister. And so some are called, and educated, and set apart.

We have considered, then, two aspects of the question who *is* a minister in our Way? If, however, laymen have such an important share in our ministry, how are we to regard the professional minister? What is his place among his people? His life among us is utterly different from that of priests of the Roman or other episcopal orders. He wears no garb to set him apart from other men. He is not called "Father" to be raised above other men. He is pastor, friend, and brother. He dresses as his people dress, he lives as they live, he walks where they walk, for he is one with them.

In his preaching of the Word, he stands before his people not even as a man, and much less as a priest above them. The gown of black he wears is, in fact, to blot him out so that his Word may be heard. He comes to us as John the Baptist once came, declaring, "I am a *voice* crying in the wilderness, prepare ye the way of the Lord." Only a voice. The voice of a lonely, faithful man telling the world the Word he has heard from God.

For the Romans, their priest is a higher order of human being. He is a step above his people on the spiritual ladder. He is not subject to quite the same punishments in the after-life as his people. He is set apart in every way, in dress, in greeting, in doctrine, and in deference. His Church believes that to it Christ's authority has been given; that it has been preserved and passed down through ages in an apostolic succession of bishops; that it is an authority held by the hierarchy and represented to the people in the person of their priests. To them, then, this man—their priest —actually *has* Christ's authority. He speaks for Christ. He acts for Christ.

But we, and all the reformation churches, say that the only authority for the Christian is Christ Himself. The Church cannot usurp His power. He still lives. He still acts. He still is present among his people.

We *have* no priest who can turn bread into flesh, and wine into blood! Our minister acts only in the Name of Christ. He has no authority. Any power he has, any gifts, any virtues, are Christ's power, Christ's gifts, Christ's virtue. The minister in a free church is only an instrument. A vessel that, pray God, Christ is sometimes able to use. And he is an instrument in the same sense that all his people are instruments. He is a man, as they are men. He is no better, no different. He is one deacon with all the other deacons, one sinner "standing in the need of prayer" with all the other sinners.

Again the black robe of a free church minister is not to set him apart nor to raise him up in beautifully embroidered ecclesiastical finery. It is an academic gown. Its only ecclesiastical significance is the one already mentioned, of blotting him out. Even the hood he may wear is an academic hood. Such a robe, if it means anything, bears testimony to our continuing regard for an educated ministry.

And yet there is a different kind of dignity which the finest ministers of our Way possess. It is a dignity that does not depend upon deference by law, nor upon hierarchical backing, nor clerical dress. It is the dignity of an inner integrity. It is the dignity that comes from faith, the grace that is given by prayer. If a man in the ministry has this kind of honesty, if he has stood humble before God, and has walked with the Master, then among the people he serves he is known as a friend, is heard as a prophet, and is respected as a man of God. To the people of our Way, this is enough.

One final note must be added on who is a minister in Congregationalism. To say that ministers are of the people, and that all the people are ministers does not tell the whole story. It is part of our faith, as Congregationalists, that within the priesthood of all believers the minister does not even have exclusive claim on those functions which are his by profession.

Lay people are not only called to care for the sick and to love the brethren. In the early Church, some of the greatest preachers were laymen, some of the wisest counselors were never ordained. And so the Congregational Way has always kept open its mind and its heart to welcome to the pulpit and even to the table those men of gifted spirit who come to life now and then in all of our churches.

The Lay preacher—how nearly unknown he is in America and how necessary and needed in Britain: faithful, willing laymen who can honestly and in truth break the Bread of Life Sunday after Sunday to their brother Christians in some little out-of-the-way chapel that cannot afford a minister. In our Way a layman can preach, and in the absence of the pastor, as a deacon of the church can quite appropriately minister at the Table of the Lord.

Article XIII of Savoy states that

> "Although it be incumbent on Pastors and Teachers of the Churches to be instant in Preaching the Word, by way of Office; yet the work of Preaching the Word is not so peculiarly confined to them, but that others also gifted and fitted by the Holy Ghost for it, and approved (being by lawful ways and means in the Providence of God called thereunto) may publiquely, ordinarily and constantly perform it; so that they give themselves up thereunto."

It is also a measure of our openness to the spiritual gifts of the gathered people, that the words "there is neither Jew nor Greek, bond nor free, male nor female" are taken seriously even in regard to the ministry. Congregationalism has pioneered in America in the Ordination of women to the ministry of the churches.

Here again, it is not law or tradition that finally counts in the life of the gathered church. It is the power of the Spirit, the "gracious calling of the Lord," and the willingness of His people to entrust their lives to Him, and to follow the leading of this Spirit wherever it may move into the ways of truth, and of new life.

We have considered how one comes to *be* a minister, and who actually is a minister. It remains to consider what is the preacher's task. Much, in passing, has been already said, but look for a moment at some of the great tasks that face those who are "raised up to minister."

First, always first, is *the task of preaching*. There are some in Protestantism who say that the day of preaching is over. "Let prayer, and scripture, and song be our ministry," they say. "Tone down the preaching. Preaching is out of hand— just a cult of personality. We've had too much of it." But many have a deeper fear: "Why! We just can't compete. How can you expect people to come and just hear a man talk when television, movies, and slick magazines are about them on every hand? We cannot match competition like that!"

Can't we? There is nothing that all the television and movies and magazines in the world have invented which can beat a man talking. Especially if it is a man with a message, a man with the power of the Spirit running through and through his life until he is on fire with Good News, and his fire lights other fires in the hearts of his hearers. There is no substitute for that, and people will go a long way to find it. Again and again this happens—people will follow the man who speaks Christ to their souls.

It is wrong in so many ways. Yet in one way it is right. It is right if it can show us that it is preaching that is needed, preaching that has been neglected, preaching— great preaching—that the world is literally dying to hear.

Congregationalism was once a preaching tradition—and still is. Yet, the old fire is gone from so many pulpits. We have outstanding administrators, excellent fund-raisers, some great pastors, but so few great preachers. The danger always—especially in a day of managers and manipulators —is to strain to the top not the great spirits, but the successful salesmen; not the men with a passion, but the solid citizens; not the gifted men, but the mediocre men, the uninspired and the uninspiring ones.

Preaching is the great task of the ministry today; the great task of the Church—and certainly of our Congregational churches. For how are the gathered people to know the power of the Spirit unless they hear His Word in the Bible and in the voice of a man? We are a "people of the Word." Our very life depends upon our hearing that Word. In our Way, we have nothing else to lean upon—no law, no councils, no ecclesiastics. Only Christ. The Christ who speaks through men: the men whom He charged to "go into all the world and preach the Gospel."

We Congregationalists must recover preaching. For it is by preaching first, that we live.

The second great task of the Congregational minister is *being a pastor*. Although our claim is not exclusive, this is a peculiarly Congregational ministry. No Christian tradition can live long without it. But we are, quite probably, the denomination that would die first without it.

Because our *life* is in the congregation. We live at that point where men worship and pray, and labor and love together. And where a church is the people, where men and women with all their human failings and problems are all that we have to lean on and work with, the ministry of a faithful pastor is both a blessing and desperate necessity.

Where people count so much they must be visited: visited until friendship grows, until hearts are opened, until prayer is possible. In the Congregational Way, the people's pastor is their one link with all their fellow-Christians. He is like the hub of the wheel binding his flock close by the radiating spokes of his love and care.

Dr. Alexander White of Free St. George's, Edinburgh, often exclaimed to young ministers: "Get into the homes of your people!" Here is where people are really known—here against their own background and among the people and the tensions that make up their life.

Hear how Savoy charges the preacher to be a shepherd seeking for the lost children of men. In Article XIV, it says of preachers that they "ought not to neglect others living within their Parochial Bounds, but besides their constant publique Preaching to them, they ought to enquire after their profiting by the Word, instructing them in, and pressing upon them the great Doctrines of the Gospel, even personally and particularly, so far as their strength and time will admit."

Counseling in the office, I am convinced, can never do this. In a day so busy that pastors of every tradition are tempted to set themselves up as counselors instead of seeking the lost in the home, we—of all people—should be telling the world that one task of the ministry is being a pastor.

The third great task of the ministry among us is *the task of praying*. Perhaps this is assumed, but it never should be, for ministers, like other men, can become poor in prayer.

Prayer is the task that comes first for every Christian. For the minister, it is here that all the doors are opened for whatever else he would do—especially for great preaching and great pastoring. It is the force that can change lives, deepen spirits, and transform souls and bodies. It is through prayer that the way of the Gospel itself is prepared.

Most of us ministers do not spend enough time at prayer.

But we must. For it is prayer, if anything, that can cast fire in the heart of the Church. Our great task is *praying for people.* One of Scotland's great preachers made it always a practice in his parish to take a half-dozen families of his church into prayer each day. He took them before God and prayed for them. And often people, not knowing, came to ask if they had been prayed for—they had received such blessings! This is the least we can do.

But we can also ask to be used in *Christ's ministry of healing.* Always this was His charge: "Preach, and heal." We hang back from this. This is fearful indeed, and what man would not tremble before it. Yet it is the province of ordinary men. Peter surely was such, and Jesus' own love could not help but heal.

Is not there a place in the ministry of the Congregational Way for the laying-on-of-hands and its ministry to the sick? The Spirit is power: power in the midst of every gathered congregation. We dare not hold it back, nor refuse to follow where He would lead.

To that end, we must also *be teaching the people to pray.* They do not know as much as we think. We can assume nothing—especially in a Congregationalism that has had recently more than its share of rationalism.

Family prayer, personal prayer, and the great prayers of faith and healing—all these the churches of the Congregational Way must learn if they are ever to be people of the Spirit, gathered around a Christ whom they long to hear and believe. It is in prayer that He speaks, and in prayer that men seek. And who shall "teach us to pray" if not the one ministering in the name of Him Who is the end and the very strength of prayer?

Preaching, pastoring, praying—this is the ministry of

the Congregational Way. A thousand other demands always are made and the people must learn *not* to make them. For these three are the great tasks to which our ministers are called, the tasks that count the most, and most truly serve the Master.

The ministry, in whatever denomination, is a terrifying calling. It is a calling which no man dare answer without fear and trembling. And among us in Congregationalism, it is both the most exalted office and the most common duty.

Those who are called to live this life are called to a paradox. Their privilege is the pulpit, and the Table, and the hearts of their people. But their calling is, too, to be one of those people. If he can live with these both—the wonder and the humility—then the minister in our Way is one of the most greatly blessed among men.

8. The Way of the Spirit

One of the great realities of life in the Christian Church is that everything we are trying to do is in the realm of the ideal. We follow a Christ Who walks the high-roads of a life we can scarcely glimpse from our uncertain path on the lowland plain. We strive to be what we know we never shall become. We try to serve lost lives as the Master did, when feeling all the while the sin of selfishness keeping us from His utter sacrifice. We work to be a community of love, yet know full well the little resentments and hypocrisies that are harbored within the Church. We believe our mission is to win all men to Christ, and yet we know they will not listen, and that we, too, will grow weary in well-doing.

We are involved every day of our lives in such terrible impossibilities. We grow so used to speaking in noble phrases, in saying such glowing, helpful things, and yet secretly expecting so pitifully little to actually happen. We try so hard to stir each other up, to work up enthusiasm for our pet projects and our great ideas, and our amazement is that some still listen, still believe.

This book on Congregationalism must seem to be just so

much more of exactly the same. The whole picture is an ideal: the dream that thrilled our fathers' hearts; the hope that carried their spirits back to the excitement of the earliest church's life; the passion that fired their hearts to live a rebel life in the land they loved, and finally to build their Way on the barren coasts of a wilderness land. It is a dream, a hope, a passion, but how much of a reality? How real have all these dreams become in the life of our Congregational Way? How well do we even understand these hopes our fathers had, the meanings they saw in the covenant-life of the gathered people? How determined are we to live and make relevant in our day the christian life that was their vision so long ago?

We Congregationalists of modern America are heirs of a heritage that has long been forgotten. We live with the memory of a great tradition and yet we are no longer sure just what it is. A word here and a word there have come down to us and we carry them as little banners; but they are not the whole truth, they are not the glorious fulness of *Christ's* banner "floating o'er us."

Curiously, we live in a day that is hungering for greatness. Through all around us that is cheap and mass-produced, through the hidden persuasion and the insidious conformity, through all the false enjoyments and the drummed-up excitement there is an honest yearning for what is sincere, for that which has integrity, for things which are great, and powerful, and moving.

I believe that the new interest in religion in our land is a sign God has given us that men are looking for this greatness in the *Church*. I do not pretend to say that they are looking for it especially in *our* church Way or that I think it can only be found here. Wherever churches gather men are looking for this quality: looking for a Word to be spoken, a life to be lived, a Lord to be revealed. They do not care in what church they find it. They care only that this thing they are looking for be found *somewhere*, in some church. Indeed, modern men would as soon forget about denominations, and about their differences which seem to them petty, and press through to the eternal Christ Who should be present in all of them.

What I have been trying to say all through this book is that our Way was so conceived by our Congregational fathers that it would have this greatness—that it would be embodied in our very life. Back in their seventeenth century days of vision they saw straight through all the magic and machinery of medievalism to an early Christian life in which all the trappings were cut away and Christ alone stood powerful and real at the heart of the Church. They saw men and women meeting in Corinth and Antioch, Rome and Thessalonica to share a blessed fellowship with Christ and His friends. They saw those early saints and martyrs asking no creeds or credentials of those who gathered, but only that they believe in Christ as their Lord and be eager to live the Resurrection-life of His people. They saw them living by love, disciplined by faith, and powered by hope: not needing the bonds of ecclesiastical dogma and decree because they were bound to Christ and free in Him. They saw the life of covenant-love those early Christians were living. They saw how the Lord Christ's Spirit moved in that fellowship, binding them close. They saw how each man counted and was loved because he was one of the brethren. All these things our forebears saw, and knew that the life they wanted to live must *also* be bound to this Christ in the same kind of covenant-community. It was from this vision that the Congregational Way was born.

I have tried to say that, although the profound understanding has been lost, although we have remembered and clung to only bits and snatches of what our fathers saw, there still lies treasured up in this heritage of our past a greatness that the future needs. Christ can be known in our Way. He can work wonders of grace through the freedom that is ours. He can use the Meeting, and the Covenant, and the eager openness of our Way to make us the church of greatness for which so many hearts hunger.

But if this is to happen we must be different from what we are now. We know this. We feel in our own lives that something is missing. We hear of a man throwing away his life to be a doctor in Africa and we know inside, "That's not for me, I wouldn't dare." Or a young person in school loses most of her friends because she stands for her faith, and we wish her well but we never stand with her. Or we see a person burdened with all the suffering this world can give and come out singing, and we stand back amazed, knowing deep in our souls, "This couldn't be me, I haven't the faith!"

We are Christians, we are regularly in church, we give to its work, we serve on its committees, and yet deep down we know there is something that we lack. We know there are Christians who possess a quality of faith that we do not even understand. We wonder if this is the reason why—even with so many fine people in our churches—greater things do not happen in our midst.

We read about Pentecost, with that great congregation stunned by the words of a Peter, and overcome by the power of the Spirit. We read of Paul, journeying tirelessly around the Roman world telling his magnificent message wherever men would listen. We read of Stephen, dying in a hail of stones, with his face shining like the face of an angel; and of that entire early Church on the march, moving with a power from beyond itself, sweeping everything before it until the Empire itself owned its sway: until Constantine the Great rode at last under the sign of the Cross; until market and palace, Senate and rude homes were hearing everywhere the one name, Jesus Christos; until a whole new people of God had risen up and begun to live with the light of the glory of this Christ shining in their lives.

Why, we wonder, isn't our church like this? And why do not we, as Christian people, live this way? Why aren't we holding high the Cross of Christ, and preaching the Gospel, and healing the sick as these people did, and as Christ charged us to do?

There is an answer, and we who profess to be Christians of the Congregational Way are the ones who should know what it is. Because even in the New Testament there were people who wondered about this. The answer is given in the Book of Acts in a most interesting story—really, two stories—about this problem of living our faith.

The first is the story of a man named Apollos. Apollos was one of the greatest preachers of the first-century Church: eloquent, sincere, moving, and powerful. He was a Jew who knew the Old Testament Scriptures, who had heard about Jesus, and who, as the story says, "taught diligently the things of the Lord."

He had been baptized by John, and like John both his baptism and his message were of repentance—of repenting for sin and determining to do good. And yet when Priscilla and Aquila—those wonderful church workers we hear of so often in Paul's letters—heard him, they realized that something was missing. He had everything—power, poise, knowledge, everything—except the Spirit of Christ upon him. Priscilla and Aquila then took him aside and told him this Good News which somehow he had not heard and was not preaching.

The second part of the story is a similar incident in which Paul met certain disciples in Ephesus with whom again, something was missing. Paul asked them what would seem to us a rather strange question: "Have ye received the Holy Spirit since ye believed?" And their answer, perhaps even more amazing, was that "We have not so much as heard whether there *be* a Holy Spirit." They had not even heard! So Paul laid his hands on them and they received the Holy Spirit and began to "speak in tongues" and to "prophesy."

In both cases—with lay people, and with a great preacher —perfectly sincere and devout Christians had been missing something vital and crucial in their faith, even though they had been Christians a long time.

I wonder if this story does not say something very important to all of us who call ourselves Christians of the Congregational Way? Perhaps the one question we need most critically to be asked is Paul's question, "Have ye received the Holy Spirit since ye believed?"

Upon first hearing, these Ephesians were probably a little suspicious of Paul. "Who is this fellow with his strange idea about a holy spirit?" Had they been able to, they might well have shut the door or turned their backs upon him. Their answer was, "We have not so much as heard whether there be any Holy Spirit!"

This all sounds rather like the question some of us have

been asked, "Are you saved, brother? Have you received the Holy Spirit since ye believed?" This embarrasses us. We call ourselves Christians, and yet we know that if we were to answer the question honestly many of us would have to say no—"No, we have not received the Holy Spirit."

It is especially embarassing to us Congregationalists, for the reputation we have developed over the years is of a rather cold, rational, intellectual sort of faith. We have tended to put stock in man's rational capacities to save himself and to change the world by his own strength rather than by God's.

The idea of the Holy Spirit sounds to us like an altogether different kind of religion. Not for us, we think. This is not the respectable, safe religion that *we* know about! No, leave all this to the fundamentalists, and the pentecostals—"We have not so much as heard whether there be any Holy Spirit!"

But the apostle Paul was not a man easily satisfied. His rejoinder to the Ephesians was this: "Unto what baptism then, were ye baptized?" This is the real question. What has our baptism meant to us? What did it do to us? How did it change us? And if we were baptized as infants, what has happened to us since that gives us the right to call ourselves Christians?

What, actually, has being a Christian meant to us all these years? For many people today, joining a Congregational church is too easy. It is just one of those things you do that makes you a member; that includes you as part of the organization. But it is not life-changing; it is not one of those high moments when the heavens open, and the Spirit descends upon us, and we know that our lives will never be the same again.

And yet it ought to be. Baptism is the one great moment

of life when God claims us for His own: when He chooses us and gives His seal that we are His and always have been His, from the foundation of the earth.

The trouble is that most of us have been living like those Ephesian disciples, as if ours were simply "John's Baptism" of repentance. We have been living as if all our religion means is that we are simply to give up our bad habits and try to be good. We Congregationalists, along with most other Christians, have been satisfied with this half-Gospel too long. This is only the beginning of what our faith should be!

The *Good News* is that Jesus Christ is risen from the dead, that He rolled away the stone of death forever, that He bore the sins of men on Calvary's cross, and that He has stormed the very gates of heaven to win our salvation and to bring us back new life. Christianity is victory. It is a singing, conquering faith that makes a shambles of fear with its truth that "perfect love casteth out fear"; that pierces the heart with its warning that "he who says he loves God but hateth his brother is a liar . . ."; that cures the plague of worry with its "be not anxious for tomorrow"; that lifts up loneliness with its wonderful testimony that "The Lord is my shepherd I shall not want"; and defeats even sorrow with its question: "Who shall separate us from the love of God?"

Christianity means living in the power of the Holy Spirit. It means receiving that Spirit into our lives and being made into new creatures by it. It means losing all those burdens of worry and fretfulness, sin and guilt which we so often insist upon carrying, but which Christ came to carry for us. It means being healed of our diseases and cleansed from our unrighteousness. It means having a

Christ to live for, and knowing the confidence, and joy, and peace which He alone can give.

This is the difference between the Christians who have spiritual power in their lives, and those who do not. They have "received the Holy Spirit." It is as simple as that: somewhere, somehow, they have received this gift which every one of us needs.

It is this life which we of the Congregational Way have been called to live. This is the witness we were meant to make. This is what we can be when we receive this Spirit of our Lord and Christ.

It is when we have received Him that our churches will begin to live the life touched with greatness for which the men of our time are seeking.

Perhaps, when that day comes, we will not care so much to do everything with speed, to be only efficient, to be ecclesiastically "successful." Perhaps, in that day, we will have learned to wait quietly, to gather in the Meeting with our covenant-brothers, to listen patiently with them for the Word of our Lord, and to find Him among us in power and in love.

Bibliography

A *Book of Worship for Free Churches*, New York: Oxford, University Press, 1948.

Atkins, Gaius Glessn, and Fagley, Frederick L., *History of American Congregationalism*, Boston and Chicago: The Pilgrim Press, 1952.

Walker, Williston, *The Creeds and Platforms of Congregationalism*, New York: Scribner, 1893.

Walker, Williston, A *History of the Christian Church*, Edinburgh: T. & T. Clark, 1949.

Willson, George F., *The Pilgrim Reader*, Garden City: Doubleday & Co., Inc., 1953.

Index